LET'S TALK ABOUT EPILEPSY

LET'S TALK ABOUT ABOUT EPILEPSY

ANN MARIE GILLIE

TRULY INSPIRING STORIES

outskirtspress
DENVER, COLORADO

Outskirts Press, Inc.
http://www.outskirtspress.com

ISBN: 978-1-4327-8797-4

Outskirts Press and the "OP" logo are trademarks belonging to Outskirts Press, Inc.
PRINTED IN THE UNITED STATES OF AMERICA

Dedicated to
My Facebook Epilepsy Support Group

"Life isn't about finding yourself, it is about creating yourself"
–George Bernard Shaw

癲癇 Epilepsia Epilepsi

EPILEPSY

It comes in every language!

Farfajiya

Epilepszia

Tutarağ

Table of Contents

Introduction

Writing **Let's Talk About Epilepsy** came about for me after getting such an amazing response from my first book, **If Walls Could Talk: Don't let epilepsy control you!** In this new book I am very pleased and honored to share some incredible stories from others that also made a life altering decision, which was to have brain surgery.

It is amazing how similar we all are and it doesn't matter our ages, nationalities or where we live in the world; we seem to have a bond with one another and it feels great! Along with some personal experiences with epilepsy, I passed out some questions for whoever chose to answer them, questions like; how many different meds have you been on for your seizures? Did epilepsy affect your education, either elementary, high school or college/university? Did or does having epilepsy affect any specific relationships in your life? Have you ever gone for a second opinion? I had some great answers to all these questions; I did throw my own answers in as well, of course!

I think the inspiration in this book is going to help those out there that struggle with epilepsy in their own life; it is unfortunate that not everyone has a place to go, talk or feel safe in when it comes to their epilepsy or seizures, but I hope after reading these incredible stories that you will find a place, or support group that fits what you need; that your life will become more positive than you could of imagined. I know from my own personal experience that support is the key when it comes to almost everything in one's life, sometimes we just might need a bit of a nudge to get it!

When I was in Phoenix in 2010 I got a tattoo on the inside of my right arm that says **BELIEVE** and that is something I do every day now and will continue to do so; if a person doesn't have **anything** to believe in than the world can be a pretty empty place and we all deserve the best in life!

BELIEVE in yourself!

CHAPTER 1

Where am I today? I am on top of the world!

What is the true meaning of "**being inspired**"? Is it being motivated or stimulated by something that has happened in your life, or maybe you were moved by an experience you witnessed someone else to have. There are allot of reasons that people's lives are inspired or changed and sometimes we just don't take the time to sit back and reflect on them.

I was inspired to write my first book after a life changing experience I had in December 2002 when I underwent neuro surgery for my seizures at the University of Alberta Hospital in Edmonton, Alberta. My surgery was an absolute success; it changed my life forever and has given me a different perspective on life. My surgery was called Left Selective Amygdalohippocampectomy and to this day is something I talk about, write about and reflect on as if it happened yesterday.

December 2009 is when I had my first book *If Walls Could Talk: Don't let epilepsy control you!* published, from that I became more involved in public speaking than ever before, I was given opportunities to speak in places I would never of imagined. One speaking engagement that is still probably the most inspiring one for me was when I was the guest speaker at the *Phoenix Arizona Epilepsy Walk April 2010*. I wasn't sure how many people would actually be attending the walk, I was thinking at least 400 maybe 500, I never really asked beforehand what their numbers usually were every year. Well I was way off, there were over 1200 people! It was amazing for me, exciting, a little overwhelming but a highlight in my speaking for sure.

I was the guest speaker at the Phoenix Epilepsy Walk in Phoenix, Arizona April 2010

The attention I received from people at the walk was so uplifting and rewarding. I had small children approach me like I was a celebrity, I loved it! One of the questions I got from a little girl who was about 6 or 7 was, "do you live in an igloo?", I just laughed and said no it does get very cold where I live and we do have winter ½ the year but I live in a house like you. She was so cute. After the walk I got the opportunity to speak with others that were there and I loved the questions and enthusiasm these people had when it came to talking about their epilepsy experiences. We compared different medications we had all taken, treatments and where we are today as far as our seizures went. I am still very pleased to say that I have been 110% seizure free since my surgery back in 2002.

Through my speaking engagements thus far, I have come to the conclusion that life is what we make of it, we choose different directions to go in, but ultimately we are in charge of our own destinies. We can't always please everyone in our lives, whether it is friends, family, co-workers or neighbors, but we can always build on it. I personally have come a long way since having my surgery over nine years ago that cured my seizures, I am constantly surprising myself with ideas I come up with and it feels great. I have a zest for life that seems to grow stronger all the time.

My Second Phoenix Walk - 2011

Have I changed since the surgery? Definitely!! However change is good in anyone's life, we sometimes need to alter or make things different in order to move forward. When I was at my 4 year old son Nathan's yearly check up last august, we were sitting in the room waiting for his doctor to come in and I saw a quote on the calendar that I just can't seem to get out of my head. It said *"**Life isn't about finding yourself, it is about creating yourself**"*. Since reading that I have run it through my head thousands of times and I want to learn how to create myself in a way that pushes me to do my best, to look at life in only positive ways. So for me sitting back down and writing another book really is another form of creating.

I have been in touch with several individuals on my *Life After Brain Surgery* Group on Facebook and I asked how many would be interested in sharing their stories with me for this book. Well I was overwhelmed with the response, it was incredible, so many came forward and said they would love to share their epilepsy stories. So after chatting and talking with a handful of great people on my Facebook group I put together some incredibly uplifting stories to share with you. It is always good to hear different points of view from others going through similar situations, as we are all different, but at the same time we do share one thing in common; we beat a huge obstacle in our lives, Epilepsy. I hope their stories touch you like they touched me!

My middle son Cameron, who is 13 yrs old is a story writer himself and I asked him if he would be willing to do some writing with me in this book, to share his story of living with a mom that had seizures and how my life with epilepsy affected him personally. So Cameron agreed to do so, but he wanted to do it on his own without any help from me. I definitely have to give him credit for even taking that task on, thanks Cameron! My oldest son Mathew along with my parents also offered to share a page with you, on their thoughts about me and epilepsy. I really appreciate all of them wanting to share their thoughts with all of you. Thank you!

If you read my first book you would have read some things about my experience after surgery that weren't as enlightening as they are in this book, I went through some pretty frightening times with depression and speaking about it in my book was a huge lift to get me out from where I was. People need to talk, need to express how they feel. If we hold everything in and think it will all go away on its own that we are only kidding ourselves. Now I won't get into detail here like I did in *If Walls Could Talk,* I just want others to know that "hey I made it through and you can to". So if I went back to my surgery, which was just over 9 years ago now and listed what events or obstacles, even achievements

I have encountered, I must say I have quite a list; so saying that, I suppose I better share some of them with you.

Here it goes –

- My neuro surgery was Dec 2002.

- Went back to school and got my certification for Emergency Medical Dispatch in 2003.

- Started public speaking in 2004

- Wrote my first book 2009

- As far as surgeries go, I had a few, but not anywhere above the shoulders.

    - Tubal reversal (which worked 100% to, I got pregnant with Nathan exactly one year after the surgery), than had a hysterectomy – **NO MORE BOYS** for me!!

    - Tore my Achilles playing soccer in January 2011, had surgery a few days after the tear, than the week of Mothers Day in May 2011, I ended up in for emergency surgery on my Achilles and had 3 more surgeries that week… and all I wanted to do was play soccer again. Maybe I should stick to writing; I don't think I can get hurt doing that! I am still recovering but definitely not healing even close to as well as I did from my neuro surgery back in 2002.

After everything my body has been through I am still hanging in there, it just seems to be taking longer to heal, does that come with age? Please don't answer that. I promised myself that I will get back on the soccer field as soon as I am 100% healed; I just can't risk tearing it again.

Near the end of this book I list a bunch of different events or forums that I have had the opportunity to speak at. One in particular, that had a huge impact on me, is when I got to see my surgeon for the first time in years. In March 2010 I was asked to be a speaker at the Glenrose Auditorium in Edmonton, Alberta on the topic of Seizures and Surgery.

My surgeon from Dec 2002 was also a speaker and I was so excited to go up and speak with him that I was almost speechless; yes me speechless. He changed my life. I brought my book **If Walls Could Talk** along to give to him, I even signed it, I wanted to show my gratitude, my appreciation for all he has done for me and how he changed my life. I will always be indebted, always! I was trying to think of what I can say to him to let him know how I really feel, and the two words that came out of my mouth, which were simple, but to me how I felt, were *Thank you.*

Another very inspiring talk or day for me was actually quite recent; it was in October 2011 in Calgary, Alberta, where I was the guest speaker that evening at the Calgary Epilepsy Association. People don't realize sometimes what an impact they can make on others, maybe we take ourselves for granted , but this speaking engagement for me was so perfect, uplifting, amazing. I was so comfortable talking about personal issues and having questions asked about everything under the sun. During the coffee break I had a few come up and ask me questions in regards to what I had just spoken about, but the one that touched me the most and still does to this very day, this minute, was a mother and father that came to talk with me with their teenage son.

They quietly came over to me and introduced themselves, said thank you for speaking about my experience and then they commented on how pleased they were that their son was asking questions. He was an awesome kid, sorry teenager, that has struggled to with seizures, meds, society, everything. Their son was someone that not only touched me but others in the room to, employees there at the association were moved as well. As I was speaking with his parents the dad was a little chocked up and I could feel what he was feeling while he was talking to me, it was one of those "clicks" that I will never forget. I love helping others, helping them see the good in what is out there. I know I don't have a magic wand or the answers to everything, but I BELIEVE that if people stick together, work together and believe that there is hope out there than we can achieve it. Maybe it won't cure things or stop them in their tracks but until you try you will never know.

**Guest Speaker at the Calgary Epilepsy Association
in Calgary, Alberta, Canada 2011**

My public speaking is my destiny and I will continue with it as long as I have the opportunities to do so. I will also continue to always thank those that have inspired me and helped me get to where I am. I hope you enjoy the stories that were sent to me for this book, I know they touched me. Just before I finished compiling all the stories sent to me for this book, and gathering all my material, I was asked by a friend if I had ever seen or listened to the documentary *The Secret*; no I hadn't, I wasn't sure what it even was. So I asked a few questions, thinking it was just another story, not really sure what it was even about or if it would even interest me.

Well was I wrong. I took the disc set with me last week when I went to Mexico, as I had a week trip booked to go with my husband, no kids, no stress, no responsibilities; there was a touch of stress, as a hurricane had just passed through the Cancun area days before we were to land, but I am a pretty positive thinker and from that we missed the closure of the airport and evacuation of the hotel by one day… yes, one day. So I was meant to go on that trip. I started listening to the first disc on the plane down there and at first it was alright, than I was hearing words and phrases that were catching my attention, words like *believe* which I had just got tattooed on my right arm last year, words like *passion, bliss, destiny;* all these words were making me feel good. That might sound a bit vague, but it feels awesome to just feel good, so I kept listening to *The Secret* and am so glad I did.

After arriving in Cancun, getting settled in the resort, having a glass of wine and relaxing I told myself I would listen to all 4 discs over this week of relaxation and I did. I wish *The Secret* would have been around years ago when I was in a not so good place, when it came to my seizures. I have always been a positive and outgoing person, but I feel I can accomplish what I want even more so now and I have learnt to focus on what I want and not on what I don't want, not on the negative. It was said in the story that people think there is not enough good to go around the world, that is so far from being right that it is a crazy thought.

Good is out there for all of us to experience, have and it is unlimited to the world, you just have to believe; as I am typing this I am looking at my tattoo and I do believe. *The Secret* was the *law of attraction* and we all have it, we are all creators of our own destinies, the one quote that stood out for me in *The Secret* was from Robert Collier, he said "all power is from within and is therefore under our control". We all have the power we just need to find it. I found the power to get out there in the world and share my life experiences with other, to try and add a sense of comfort to those struggling with epilepsy and I think I am on the right path for doing so. When people work together change can happen and when positive thoughts and ideas are shared amongst people even greater things can come of it. All you have to do is **Believe**!

Ann,

"I'm a friend, a fellow employee with Ann and most of all I have Epilepsy myself. I have known Ann for just over a year, and I am so proud to be part of her life! I have never personally known anyone else with Epilepsy, never mind with the same type. Since meeting Ann I am no longer embarrassed discussing the fact that I have Epilepsy. The knowledge I have gained and the inspiration she gives to others does not go unnoticed. I would like to say thank you Ann and I look forward to reading your new book, "Let's Talk About Epilepsy".

Tanya Horton

Ann,

"Thank you so much for coming and sharing your journey through life! You are most definitely an inspirational woman!"

Calgary Epilepsy Association

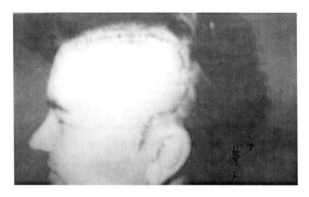

Me after my surgery December 2002!

Me NOW 2012 - 42 years old and 110% seizure free!!!

CHAPTER 2

Family

"Cameron's Page"

By Cameron Gillie

Seeing my mom have seizures for me was like going through some-thing that nobody ever wants to go through or should have to go through. It was very scary!! I know other people have gone through this before, but when it's your mom with epilepsy it's frightening, as a kid and I guess as an adult to. When she had seizures I thought she was like dying, it was that bad. I was pretty young though so don't remember allot of what my mom went through, but I do remember her seizures she had right before her surgery.

Some of them were unreal; falling on the stove, on the floor, not knowing where she was, it was crazy. When she dropped to the floor I thought she was just freaking out but it was a seizure and it got me worried. A seizure to me is like a bad heart attack for the body, it's kind of weird actually, I now know it was her brain not her heart. Allot of people don't really know what to do if they see someone having a seizure, but if you ever do see someone having one you can't let them have any items by their mouth or in their mouth because they could choke really easy; you should make them calm if you can, make sure they are safe from hurting them self and go get help. Epilepsy doesn't have to be scary for others; people just need to understand it.

I am glad my mom is better today and has no more seizures. She re-ally enjoys helping others and talking about what she went through and I think that is really cool!

Cameron Gillie

"Mathew's Page"

By Matt Gillie

My mom was having seizures way back when I was born. Being epileptic is a very serious thing, it alters one's life in way that you wouldn't think it could. Not only did it affect my mom but everyone around her, including me, my brother and allot of our family. When I was very young I didn't know how to react to a situation like if she was having a seizure, but as I grew older I realized what was happening. It was a pretty scary thing, you wouldn't know when it was coming or the severity of it, it was all very random. I was told that when I said she was having a seizure it always sounded like caesar, the drink, I made sure I pronounced it properly later on.

About 9 years ago she had a surgery on her brain to eliminate the epileptic attacks or seizures she was having, since the day of her surgery she has been 100% seizure free. She is now a public speaker for other people who have gone through what she has gone through or for those living with epilepsy. She is also the founder of a Facebook support group, that involves people all around the world who live epilepsy or that had surgery and I'm pretty sure a couple of them are in this book; these people to have gone through life changing surgeries which in the end also had the positive outcome they were hoping for.

In a way her having epilepsy changed her life for the better, she loves to help others and I think she does a great job of that!

Good work mom!

Matt Gillie

"Mom and Dad's Page"

By my parents

When we look back upon our daughter's life, we realize that one of the most important and poignant moments, was when she agreed to undergo a very delicate brain procedure called Left Selective Amygdalohippocampectomy!

At the very young age of 18 months, Ann was diagnosed with epilepsy, which was devastating news for us, simply because we knew very little about this disorder, or the potential prognosis! Even while living with, and enduring the many seizures, medication and partial paralysis, Ann's enthusiasm and activities were only tempered, not relinquished! This attitude and perseverance would be very prevalent in her adult life!

There was a long period until the age of twenty, when she was seizure free! It was at this time in her life that the seizures returned with a vengeance, leading well into her married life! Then after consultation with several medical specialists, at the age of thirty two, and with two sons Mathew and Cameron at home, the decision was made to proceed with the surgery. The medical procedure was not only a complete success, but she and her husband Richard had another son, Nathan, who was born in 2007.

Our daughter has not only continued to be a working mother of three boys, but she has been very much involved with several local organizations on a volunteer basis, including her local Epilepsy Association in Edmonton, Alberta. All of which, as her parents, we are extremely proud. She continues to show us, and many others, the same determination and enthusiasm, that she exuded as a little girl ...all those years ago.

Ann has become an excellent public speaker on behalf of Epilepsy, and has travelled to several Associations, not only in Canada, but also in the United States.

With much love, Mom and Dad

Me and my boys!!
**Mathew, Nathan, me and Cameron
(and of course Abby) 17, 4 and 13 years old**

CHAPTER 3

Epilepsy Around The World

Epilepsy is everywhere....

CANADA * USA * EUROPE * AUSTRALIA

AFRICA * ASIA * GREENLAND * HONG KONG * UK * SOUTH
AMERICA

and where you live to!!

There is close to 50 million people in the world that have epilepsy, that is a huge number, these people are of all ages right from babies to seniors, epilepsy does not target any particular age group. It is one of the oldest recognized conditions and it has unfortunately always been a disorder that has been discriminated against and never really understood by the general public. Epilepsy is a medical condition that produces seizures and is also called a seizure disorder. When someone has two or more unprovoked seizures, they are considered to have epilepsy. Seizures occur when clusters of nerve cells in the brain don't signal normally, which may briefly alter a person's movements, consciousness or actions.

Statistics

Here are some statistics and facts in regards to epilepsy:

- Epilepsy affects approx 50 million people worldwide.

- In the US there are approx 3 million - Canada 400,000 – 35 million in developing countries, with there being approx 9 million in India alone.

- Seizures are a symptom of epilepsy.

- A person having a single seizure does not necessarily mean a person has epilepsy.

- Some known causes for a person to have epilepsy are one such as brain tumors, genetic conditions and infections like meningitis.

- Epilepsy tends to responds to treatment about 70% of the time.

- Epilepsy is one of the world's oldest recognized conditions.

- Almost 90% of epilepsy cases around the world are found in developing regions.

Epilepsy Questions and Answers

What causes epilepsy?

In about 70 percent of cases there is no known cause of epilepsy, however they do know that recurring seizures can be related to:

Brain tumors and strokes * Head traumas * Poisoning * Maternal Injuries * Infections

How is Epilepsy Diagnosed?

An EEG is used to record brain waves, the electrodes are placed on the scalp; this test can detect abnormalities within the brain's electrical activity. CT (computed tomography) scans are also used and of course blood tests and a person's medical history can determine the diagnosis.

How can Epilepsy be treated?

There are several ways of treating Epilepsy but the most common are – medications, surgery and diet.

What are some of the side effects of Epilepsy medications?

Blurry vision, fatigue, swollen gums and skin rashes seem to be the most common; for myself I encountered all of those.

What is brain mapping?

It is identifying the functions of different regions within the brain. There is electrical brain mapping also, done by using direct electrical simulation on the brain.

NON drug treatments

The list of alternative therapies for epilepsy has been changing over time as new approaches keep emerging. One being the ketogenic diet, which began as an alternative therapy, but has been scientifically tested and is rapidly being accepted as a conventional therapy for patients. I have never tried the ketogenic diet myself but have heard some very good stories from those that have. Some alternative therapies do have long standing histories in some parts of the world and some are more recent developments. What they do have in common is that the safety and effectiveness of most of them have not been proven by well-designed scientific studies. Some of them may be very useful, but they must be chosen and used with care, as it is with anything.

First Aid for Seizures

1. Stay very calm!

2. Prevent the individual from causing any injury to them self by insuring there is nothing within reach that could harm the person.

3. Pay very close attention to the length of the seizure.

4. Make sure the individual is comfortable.

5. Do not hold the person down and always remember to make sure you are safe as well.

6. Do not put anything in the person's mouth!

7. It is a myth that a person having a seizure can swallow their tongue.

8. If the seizure continues for longer than five minutes, call 911 immediately!

I personally think that everyone should at some point in their lives take first aid, as you never know when you might need it!

Different Surgeries

(Brief descriptions on a few different surgeries)

Temporal Lobectomy

It is the removal of a portion of the temporal lobe and is the most common type of epilepsy surgery; it also is considered the most successful type of surgery.

Frontal Lobectomy

It is the removal of a portion of a frontal lobe and is considered the second most common type of epilepsy surgery.

Parietal and Occipital Lobectomy

The parietal and occipital lobes are located in the back of the brain, a parietal lobectomy or occipital lobectomy is surgery to remove part of one of these lobes.

Hemispherectomy

It is disconnecting one side of the brain, that is, one cerebral hemisphere from the rest of the brain.

Corpus Callosotomy

Is when the corpus callosum is cut.

Multiple Subpial Transections

If partial seizures originate in areas of the brain that cannot be removed safely than a multiple subpial transections is an alternative.

Deep Brain Stimulation

It is an experimental therapy in which a stimulating electrode is implanted in the brain itself.

CHAPTER 4

Inspiring Epilepsy Stories

*Australia * USA * Canada * UK*

A special thank you to those that took the time to share their epilepsy experiences with all of us! You are amazing people!

Monique Laurin from *Canada*

I have knowingly lived with Epilepsy since I was 19 when I was diagnosed after a grand mal seizure in 1989. From 1989 until 2010 I took at least 6 different medications or combinations of to control my complex partial seizures (absence seizures). I've never had any auras or memory of experiencing an absence seizure which made it impossible for me to know if I had a seizure when I was alone. I only knew I'd had a seizure when someone told me what had happened. Realizing this made me wonder if I'd been having seizures prior my diagnosis in 1989.

During this time I've lived on my own and attended two post-secondary institutions obtaining a diploma and a degree. I've also played sports and led a 'normal' life. My epilepsy has never prevented me from doing what I've wanted to. The only impact I've experienced was having to take transit instead of driving when I was changing medications and during the testing process. I have experienced side effects from some of the medications.

I started on Tegretol and had pretty good control (that I know of) but gained about 30 lbs. We switched over to Topamax but had to add Clobazam (Frisium) for insurance for quite a few years. The weight came off, but over time I developed kidney stones and would have an attack approximately every 6 months. After approximately 5 or 6 attacks we decided to change the meds. That's when we replaced the Topamax with Trileptal (a sister drug to Tegretol) which resulted in weight gain again. The decision was made in 2008 to remove the Trileptal and try a higher dose of Clobazam. I did not have 100% control of the seizures so Keppra was added to the mix.

Fortunately in about 2007 I started researching surgery as an option. That's when I came across Ann Gillie's successful experience of being seizure and medication free for 5 years (at that time) after having had surgery. There is definitely a higher power at work because Ann worked part time at my ringette team's home rink and her surgery had been performed at a local hospital that has an epilepsy clinic. On December 31, 2008 I requested a referral to the clinic from my neurologist. After having met with a neurologist at the clinic, undergone telemetry and neuropsychological testing, and having my case reviewed by a panel of doctors at the clinic I was approved for surgery in December 2009.

I was given the option of going straight for surgery or having further testing (depth probes) done to better pin-point where the seizures were originating. After having talked to the surgeon in February 2010 I opted to head straight to surgery. I found out after the meeting that the waiting period for the depth probe test was approximately 1 year. I underwent a right temporal resection in April 2010. I consider myself very lucky to have had the same neurologists and surgeon as Ann.

Prior to having surgery I was informed that there was a slight chance of my visual memory being affected. I am fortunate that the only noticeable side effects from the surgery are being more talkative and more emotional. Some say I've gone through a personality change. I can handle that considering I've had brain surgery. During the testing process I was fortunate to have awesome teammates on my ringette team that allowed me to play the entire season and not miss a game by providing me with a ride to and from the games. I was also lucky to have a large and supportive circle of extended family and friends, Ann being probably my biggest supporter/mentor. I have been seizure free and am in the progress of decreasing my medications, Keppra and Clobazam. I have moved out of the City, enjoy driving around, and still doing whatever I want. I look forward to a long and healthy life, preferably medication and seizure free. Thank you Ann for sharing your story and giving me that ray of hope when I needed it as well as all the support prior to and after my surgery.

Support

One of life's necessities

Maintain

~Ann Gillie

Stacey Burns *from USA*

As any child I loved getting people's attention. Mom always said I was outgoing, motivated, and a leader. As a toddler, I was the teacher and Mom was the student or I was the mother and she was my daughter. I was always happy, positive, and full of energy. Little did I know what my life would be like as a child with epilepsy.

While growing up, I had a wonderful family. I had several sets of grandparents and great grandparents. My Mom and Dad were the best parents a girl could ask for. My first seizure started when I was about a year old. Of course, I don't remember it, but my parents said it was very frightening to see. They felt helpless and without knowing what to do, they instantly rushed me to the emergency room. During this time I had been struggling with a fever. After rushing me to the emergency room the doctors were not surprised, but they wanted to run a few test. After the testing they said I was fine and prescribed some medications. They said there was nothing to worry about and attributed to just a febrile seizure which many children have when they have a fever.

So, like any parent they listened to the doctors and thought nothing of it and for years I was your normal average girl. In first grade I was known as your average student, I had a few friends and loved learning. I was a little shy and quiet and liked keeping things nice, neat, and organized. My teacher was always concerned because I asked to use the restroom a lot. I had to go quite often, but then again I was only six years old. I remember having these funny feelings such as a sudden urge to pee or fear which would cause me to panic. I would jump into a fight or flight mode because I was terrified. I always wanted to hide to somehow avoid this feeling and make it go away.

Even though I had my funny moments I was your average kid who enjoyed school. I loved art class because it allowed me to use my imagination and bring it to life. I also enjoyed music; I was a part of the elementary school's choir and enjoyed learning about the instruments. In second grade I had a really hard time. I had trouble making friends, so I ended up in the bad crowd. My grades were horrible and I had a hard time paying attention in class. After having so much trouble, my parents had me switch schools. In third grade I had an amazing teacher; she would tell us she was raised in an Amish family. They allowed her to take time to discover and view the outside world then decide on her future. She went to college through this time to become an elementary teacher.

Around this time, I started having quite a few of my funny feelings in class. My teacher was very concerned so she kept an eye on me. She finally told my parents she thought I was having seizures during class. My parents set up an appointment with a neurologist. It had been a while since my doctors had seen me. The doctor decided to put me back on medication and take a few tests. I had an MRI and a small EEG so they could track my brain waves to see if and when I was having seizures. We never really seemed to have any proof that would explain, or help us understand why I was having my funny feelings or seizures.

Once my parents were aware of my possible situations, they informed my school and my teacher. This really opened their eyes. The more my family and teachers watched, the more they realized I was having more seizures then they thought. It was hard to explain to the class why I had my seizures. When I felt one coming on, I was terrified so I ran for safety. I always ran straight to my teacher. Once the seizure started, I wasn't really aware of what was going on, what my body was doing, and what I was saying, but I sure got everyone's attention. I ended up getting so much attention my classmates were jealous. This instantly caused a label for me. I was a special child. My classmates were so scared of me their only reaction was "get away from us." I was now standing out like a sore thumb. I was picked on and made fun of. I was a "freak" and a "monster."

They started teasing and picking on me. If they did talk to me, they would ask if I was possessed. It was hard being a child. I had a hard time making friends. It was hard being myself around other students at school. Outside of school, I had a few friends in our neighborhood who understood. They were aware I had seizures, but they had never seen me have one. I always managed to have them at school and sometimes in my sleep. I continued taking my medication proscribed by the doctor. It appeared to be helping. My doctor believed I was going to grow out of them, probably during puberty. My sixth grade year was my first year of middle school. I enjoyed being in choir and I had a few close friends. After elementary school, I had a hard time trusting people. I was known as a quiet girl or the listener. I was so hurt, ashamed, and embarrassed of my seizures I wasn't about to open up to others. I started to feel helpless and alone.

Around this time my great grandfather passed away. I remember attending his showing and funeral, but as a child it was hard to understand what was truly happening. The family talked about what they should do with his house after he passed away. They finally decided to give his house to my parents. So, it wasn't long before we started packing, and planned moving. I was pretty upset that we were moving. I didn't like the idea of moving and change. I didn't want to switch school and lose what friends I had. I had always attended large schools. Now we were moving to a small country town where my father was raised. That summer was the most boring summer, because I didn't know anyone. I later found out there were hardly any students on our end of town. A lot of them lived out in the country. I did have an advantage coming from a larger school. I had already attended junior high and I got used to having a locker and remembering my combination. In the larger schools you had to book it to get to class on time to avoid tardiness. I finally realized this was my chance to start over. No one had to know about my seizures.

Now that I was on medication my seizures were pretty minimal. I figured no one had to know I have seizures. I thought it was worth a try, hiding them for a while. Finally I got to a point I could not hide them anymore. I would always run for my teachers hoping to get their attention before it was too late. Well, I had their attention all right. I got everyone's attention. So much for hiding them and it wasn't long before they were no longer a secret. I remember bits and pieces during my seizures. My teachers would call the nurse, once they were aware I was going into the seizure. Sometimes they would have two or three students help guide me to the nurse's office.

After I went into my seizures I had no control over my body. My classmates were trying to be supportive and helpful by gently guiding me towards the nurse's office. Even though I was semi aware of what was going on, my brain made the final decisions. It would send a message to my body instructing me to go against their guidance and in the opposite directions they were leading me. It was kind of pointless really. By the time we arrived at the nurse's office my seizures were usually over, and my words were starting to make since again. After I came back to reality I was exhausted and mentally tired. My nurse would have me lie down and rest. She would always call my mom to let her know I had a seizure and mom always marked her calendar to keep a log of my seizures.

Once I felt better, it was back to class. I always felt behind during school. I tried my best to catch up on what I had missed while I was gone. Even though I was the new student, I started to enjoy school. We had less than 90 students in our grade. It was a pretty small school so everyone knew everything about everyone. When I had a seizure the whole class knew. They were always understanding, but worried about my safety. For once in my life, my classmates weren't terrified of me. I finally started to fill comfortable so I started opening up. I made some really good close friends and I felt like I finally fit in. Our school was pretty bad about clicks. We had the jocks, the cheerleaders, the smart group, the artists, and the list goes on. As separated as we seemed, everyone had a big heart and during the hard times our school came together to help one another though the situation.

I always wanted to be in gymnastics, track, or play softball. I remember my freshman year of high school I peeked into softball tryouts and was terrified. I watched everyone running sprints for a minute and realized how hard they were training. I just knew the hyperventilation from heavy breathing would cause my seizures. So much for that idea, I knew softball was not right for me. So, I headed for a new direction and signed up for our high school's choir and art classes, which introduced me to poetry.

Poetry did wonders for me. It was a major stress reliever. It was my way to escape from reality. It was a way to express myself, my emotions, and dreams. I wrote several poems, which helped give me guidance while I was trying to find and understand myself. In the middle of my freshman year, I met the love of my life, my high school sweetheart. We both attended World History class together. He was the lovable, charming, handsome, comedian sitting in front of me. He always made me laugh. I couldn't stop smiling when I was around him. It was hard ending that semester, because summer began. We continued to talk through the summer. It wasn't long, summer was over and school began. We were madly in love and officially an item.

I felt so bad for him because I could only image how he felt or what was going through his head before he met my family. He was quite the gentleman and received my parent's approval. During this time, I was still ashamed and embarrassed of my seizures. I must say I was pretty talented at hiding them. I hated getting all of the attention and fighting trying to avoid going to the nurse's office. I felt it was pointless and I just wanted to be normal. I felt I was the only one who understood what my body was doing when I went into a seizure. So, I developed my own strategy to avoid all the attention and drama. When I had a warning, or aura, that my seizures were coming on, I would lay my head down, wrap my arms around my head to hide my face, and pretend I had fallen asleep. If I happen to have class with one of my close friends, I would quietly tell them my strategy and would give them a warning sign once I was going into a seizure. They knew what was going on right away and if I didn't seem to come to after a few minutes they needed to let the teacher know. Our system worked well and stopped all of the drama. I hated being separated and pushed out. I just wanted to be normal. During high school, puberty hit, my body changed, and my seizure changes. My neurologist was hoping as my hormones changed, my seizures would simply disappear. The medication was no longer working as well. My neurologist had tried to switch mediations. Either the medication had a horrible side effect or I had an allergic reaction and broke out in hives. At this point my neurologist was pretty upset and wasn't sure what else to do. So, we were referred to a specialist.

As worried as we were switching doctors, we were open to any suggestion, because it was starting to feel hopeless. At our first appointment, the specialist requested a quick 20 minute EEG test. The EEG would allow them to watch my brain waves and possibly track where my seizures were coming from. As always, I never had a seizure during the test. We figured the specialist would be upset and disappointed with the test results, but we were worried, upset, yet excited to see their outcome. After the specialist reviewed the test results, they walked toward my family and I. As they were coming closer, my heart was pounding. I just wanted to know if they saw anything, anything at all. The specialist was smiling. I didn't understand, what could they be happy about? The specialist was happy to say they saw some positive results.

The doctors finally clarified my seizures and gave us a name. They said I was having Complex Partial Seizures that were coming from my left temporal lobe. We were so excited and impressed, we were speechless. After years of tests with no results, we finally had proof. We finally had something to go off of and the specialist seemed pretty positive.

It wasn't long after the first EEG that my specialist wanted to know more so I was scheduled for more testing. MRIs, EEGs, Pet Scans, you name it, I've probably done it. As excited as I was, it wasn't long before I was frustrated again. I was sixteen years old and I didn't understand why we had to endure so much testing. I didn't understand what the doctors were looking for in the test results. I was starting to feel like a guinea pig. It was hopeless. All the family vacations, fun spring breaks, and summer with friends were disrupted. I was scheduled in and out of the hospital constantly it seemed. My specialist seemed so excited and so determined to help me, but I couldn't handle it anymore. I hit my breaking point. I was so frustrated; this was pointless, test after test after test, and still no results. For the next three years, I was in and out of the hospital.

My specialist tried new medications and more testing and nothing was working. Probably the worst of all was the Video EEGs. I felt imprisoned, stuck in the hospital for 3 to 5 days with tons of wires and electrodes glued to my head to monitor my brain wave activities. This would allow the specialist to pin point where my seizures were coming from. The doctors tried everything to make me have a seizure. They would run breathing tests to make me hyperventilate hoping to bring on a seizure. If that didn't work, they would make me stay awake for a few days and sleep deprive me and have me stare at a strobe light. The doctors would do anything to provoke my seizures and make them appear while I was at the hospital. It became so frustrating because with each test I would have no results, no seizures, nothing. I felt hopeless.

In the fall of my senior year I had it. I couldn't take any more testing. I felt I missed three years of my life and we still had no results from the tests. I was sick of being the guinea pig. I remember telling my parents that "I'm 18, I'm an adult, and I'm DONE with the testing." My parents were supportive and understanding. I continued taking my seizure medications. I tried to avoid having seizures, but there wasn't much I could do to stop them. I enjoyed the rest of my senior year. I went on our senior trip to Cedar Point. It was nice to travel and get away from home and enjoy the last chance to be with my friends. After graduation, my mom was watching out for me and talked her boss into hiring me part time during the summer at a civil engineering company she worked at for years. I worked full time through the summer and then part time once college began. It worked perfectly because mom and I worked the same hours so I car pooled with her to work. If I even felt a seizure coming on, mom was right there to protect me.

I enjoyed my summer job working with my mom, but was hoping to continue my education. At first I wanted to be an elementary teacher and minor in psychology. I loved working with children and wanted to study the brain and how it works. I just had to get my basic classes covered first then transfer from a college to a university for my bachelor degree in education. At least that was my plan. It wasn't long before my thoughts and goals had changed completely. After my first semester in college, the civil engineering company offered me a full time job with benefits including good health insurance. Part of me wanted to be young, take a risk, go to college and continue my education. The other part of me said this is your chance to taste a little piece of freedom and prove you can be independent. After thinking long and hard and weighing pros and cons, I took the job offer. I continued taking a few classes, but my direction had changed.

Now I was working full time during the day and going for business administration classes at night. One great thing about my parents, they always wanted to show that just because I had seizures doesn't mean it will stop me from anything. I can be independent. I can live out on my own. Anything is possible if you put your mind to it. Later that year, I moved out on my own. I lived in a cute, but small apartment. It was a new house that was split in two. The top half or second floor was my apartment. I had a neighbor below me on the first floor. It was far enough for me to have some independence yet close enough in case of an emergency. At this time I still was not allowed to drive. My specialist said I had to be seizure free for a year to drive.

That never happened. My Dad still made me get my driver's license just in case something bad were to happen or someone was breaking in my house and I had to run away as fast as possible. My Dad was known as the teacher and provider. My parents were always trying to prove that just because I had epilepsy it didn't mean I couldn't be myself. Mom opened some doors and provided me with a wonderful job. While Dad trained me how to drive safely if needed. I remember, Dad would tell me to stay on the wide main road with a shoulder next to me so if I felt a seizure coming on, I could pull over as soon as possible. He even trained my boyfriend back in high school how to ride with me and pull the emergency break, push the gear into neutral, and slowly guide us off the road for safety. My parents were amazing, good providers, and taught me all the basics of life that you never learn in high school or college.

My boyfriend from high school and I continued to date through college. He was going to Ball State University while I was going to Ivy Tech and working full time. We saw each other every weekend when he came home from school. We started dating in 2002, my sopho-more year of high school and continued dating through college. In 2006, we had been dating for four years now and were going out for our anniversary. It was that night, a romantic dinner, when we were having a wonderful time together that he proposed and asked me to marry him. So, of course, I said yes!

I'm proud to say he was and is the love of my life. We were engaged for two years. During this time, we were planning our wedding, while working, and going to school. We even built our first house together in May of 2007. I lived there by myself for a year and he moved in after we got married on May 10th, 2008. After our honeymoon, it was back to reality. We were newlyweds and he was continuing his education full time while working part time at night. I was frustrated and confused on what I wanted to do so I put my education on hold. It was hard being newlyweds and working opposite shifts. The only way we would get to see each other was if I stayed up late or if he was lucky enough to get home early. When he did come home, he was exhausted and just wanted to relax.

Everyone told us the first year of marriage is the hardest, but we never imagined or completely understood what they meant, but we sure do now. It took us a while to get used to our weird schedule. We barely saw each other and when we did, it wasn't very long. Missing him was driving me crazy. I hated being alone and I was miserable being stuck in the house with no way out. My friends and family were great about taking me out to eat or shopping just to get away. They did all they could to help me feel more independent yet not feel stranded. They knew how frustrated I felt feeling imprisoned and I hated being alone in case I had a seizure.

That summer, I had my usual check up with my epilepsy specialist and I asked my husband if he would come with me to the appoint-ment. One, I needed a ride and two, I wanted him to personally meet my doctors. I figured it would be the usual check up with the basic questions and process of writing normal prescriptions. I was hoping they had found a new medication because my medication was okay, but it had major side effects. I hated it. It made me feel as if there was a cloud around my head. As I would assist people at work on our deadlines, they would instruct me on my responsibilities and I always felt like it took ten seconds longer for my brain to understand what they were saying. I tried not to show my issues. In fact, I didn't tell anyone I had epilepsy until it was too late.

I remember asking my specialist if there were any new medications I could try. I thought maybe there was still a chance the medication would work. Plus, they are always finding something new, right? Little did we know this would be the doctor appointment we would never forget. There was nothing else out there. My only options were to continue taking my current medication and continue having seizures, adding a third medication which may cause more side effects, or allowing the specialist to continue the testing because she strongly believed I would be a candidate for brain surgery.

My husband and I were dumbfounded. After a few seconds, our brains processed and understood what the doctor was saying. My emotions kicked in and I balled. I could care less about brain surgery. It was the testing that terrified me. I was so sick of wasting my life, spending endless, useless nights in the hospital, and hooked up to the itchiest electrodes for days. I just remember being so frustrated and wanting to yank each and every one off my head. I couldn't take it anymore.

My specialist understood and said she would give my husband and I some time to talk it over. She was going to have a counselor stop by and help answer any of our questions. After she left, we talked and talked about it. My husband said the decision was up to me. It's my body and my choice. As soon as he said that, I realized it was my body and my choice. I had to go for it, or at least give the testing one more chance. Once the counselor came in, she was very helpful. She broke down and explained each step on what the doctors would need from us. She explained what they were looking for and why. I had already had an IQ test in high school, so all I would need is a video EEG showing three seizure activities to prove where my seizures were coming from. If I was a candidate, I would have a vision test before and after surgery to show my current vision and prove it wasn't adversely affected. If all went well, I would have one last test which would make the final decision. It would give the doctors a final result if I would be a good candidate.

My specialist was determined they were going to see results this time. She warned us, that they were taking me off the seizure medication dramatically. I was going off of it cold turkey. I was going to have withdrawals and may feel frustrated. They were going to do breathing tests to try to make me hyperventilate. If they still didn't see any results, they would have the strobe light test hoping to provoke some seizures. Then last, but not least would be deprivation. The nurses would have to come in and make sure I stayed awake, because lack of sleep is also a known cause of seizures. My specialist warned us I was not allowed out of the hospital until I they saw their results.

It was quite the battle for our first year of marriage. My husband informed his boss about the situation and was able to take off work to stay with me. My mom and dad would stop by every other night to check on how I was doing. Our grandparents would call for an update and stop in and visit as well. Even church members would stop by daily and say hello and a little prayer for results. With all the support I felt confident and just knew something had to come from this. It wasn't long that I was experiencing withdrawals. My face itched and felt funny. It felt like my face was fuzzy yet moving all at once. It drove me crazy. I became so frustrated I wanted to pull the electrodes off my head. The nurses were so sweet and dedicated. I remember them telling me they understood my frustration, but I had to leave the electrodes alone, or they would have to glue them back on, because it would affect the test results.

My friends were supportive. They stopped by to visit, or call and asked what they could bring me to eat outside of hospital food. One even stayed at our house to babysit our puggle and kitten while we were away. They even brought the Wii and video games to the hospital to keep us entertained.

For the first three days I was doing pretty well. Then finally I had had enough and broke down. It had been three days and no seizure. I wanted to leave. I was upset, angry, and disappointed. Around this time, my grandmother called. I'm not sure if she has a sixth sense or what, but she always had a feeling if and when something was going to happen. So, she called me while I was \in the middle of a breakdown and said she knew I was going to have a seizure today or tomorrow. It wasn't long and just like always, grandma was right. I went into a full blown grand mal seizure. There was an emergency button on the hospital bed that I was supposed to push if I felt one coming on. If not, my husband would. This seizure was instant and it was shocking for my husband to see. He knew it was possible for me to have them, but he had never witnessed a grand mal seizure. So, he hit the emergency button instantly to call the nurses. They rushed in and gave me a shot of valium to bring me out of the seizure.

We were now safe to say one seizure down and two more to go. I honestly don't even remember having them. When I had a seizure while I was taking my medication, they were pretty small and quick. They didn't last long. Without my medication, I would have extreme seizures with no aura or warning signs. It just all happened so fast. After all the brain wave activity, I was so physical exhausted. It wasn't long until I had a second grand mal seizure. Again my husband hit the emergency button and the nurses came running. I was given a shot to pull me out of it. Then it was rest for recovery.

I remember my parents talking to me after we told them the great news. People normally wouldn't understand why we were so excited to have seizures, but if you do have them, you would completely understand. If I was going to have them I would rather have them in the hospital with nurses near and for my specialist to see and evaluate my condition. On the sixth day, my specialist was confident on the information she received through the video EEG. She said I had a mini seizure during my sleep which gave the all the information they needed. They said I needed to have three seizures then I could go home and years and years after testing, I finally did. They would review the test and the counselor would contact me with the test results. The specialist asked the nurse to bring my medication and she ordered that I stay until my medication was back in my system before I was able to check out from the hospital.

Now was the waiting period. I tried my best to stop thinking about it. I easily stayed busy at work. It just took time for the specialist to review and make her final decision. I would remind myself the counselor said she would call once she heard the results. I just had to wait until that special phone call.

> *Ring Ring Ring! My heart was pounding. It was the hospital. Oh my, is this our results? Calm down Stacey! Don't get too excited. You're use to failure so just take a deep breath. Breathe, and answer the phone.*

"Congratulations Stacey, we have wonderful news from your test results!"

Finally, it was a success! The counselor was excited and honored to congratulate and inform us they had wonderful test results and I was a candidate for brain surgery. Our specialist was not about to waste time. She scheduled my final tests and if all went well brain surgery would take place in November.

One of my last tests was a vision test, which was pretty simple really. It was an average vision test. Each time I saw a spot or flash of light, I had to press a button and say if I saw the image left, right, top, or bottom. This was it, and we were so close. Now it was down to the final WADA test. This test would finally answer our question. It would prove if I was or was not a candidate for surgery.

After the test, we had to wait a few days to hear the results. I remember I was back at work typing away and working with the files when the phone rang. It was our counselor calling with the test results. My mom worked a cubical over and she could tell by my questions and the sound of my voice that it was my counselor calling. She ran towards my desk just waiting for our final answer. My heart pounded as

I was waiting for the answer. YES! YES! Our answer was yes! Finally, the doctors saw everything they were looking for. I was a candidate for brain surgery also known as, a temporal lobectomy. It was now down to scheduling the final date for surgery and meeting my surgeon.

When I scheduled an appointment to meet my surgeon, I asked my parents to come with my husband and I. This was going to come down to a big final decision on my part and I wanted them to be there with me. As excited as I was, I could always back out at this point. It was my body, my decision.

After meeting with the surgeon, we all felt pretty confident. He broke down and explained in detail if we decided to go through with this what would be involved. It would be a seven to eight hour surgery. They would have to shave my head, make a question mark incision, and remove a small part of brain where the test results proved my seizures started from. I would stay in ICU for two days. If all went well, on the third day I would move into the regular part of the hospital. Then I would head home for recovery.

I had to have someone with me at all times during the first five to seven days when I was home. I needed help bathing, eating, and taking medication. The first few days would be intense recovery. My surgery took place on November 18, 2008. As the surgeon said it was a seven to eight hour surgery. I stayed in the hospital for three days before I was able to head home for recovery. About a week later, I came in for a checkup appointment and the surgeon removed my staples. My hair was slowly growing back, but honestly no one could even tell. The way they shaved my head, I could still wear my hair down and hide the scar during recovery. I stayed home from work for seven weeks. I was home through Thanksgiving and by December attended each and every Christmas. Then after New Year's, I had my final checkup with my surgeon. He was pleased on how quickly I healed and to hear I had been seizures free since surgery.

After our final appointment, my surgeon gave me permission to go back to work. He suggested I try half days for a week. If it seemed fine and I felt better, I could start full time a week later. I'm proud to say I've been seizure free almost three years now. I'm still on some medication. After such success, my specialist decided to take me off one of my medications. The one thing people need to understand if you are a candidate for brain surgery is this will not eliminate taking medication. It takes medication plus brain surgery for results. Those of you, who have family, friends, or personally have a seizure disorder, you would know becoming seizure free with or without medication still means you're seizure free.

I should have never felt ashamed or afraid to be myself, but I finally realize that now. I'm no longer the shy and quite girl. I'm outgoing and out spoken and I realize there was a reason and meaning for all of this in life. I always wondered why I have epilepsy. Why was I so different when all I wanted to be was normal? Even though life was challenging, it is all clear to me now. I had my ups and downs, my anger and depression, my hopes, and my fears. This was a chapter in my life to help me understand what epilepsy was and why it takes place. After surgery I knew it was my chance to reach out and continue to educate others about epilepsy.

As soon as I could, I contacted a few non-profit organizations, the Epilepsy Foundation of Indiana and the Angels4Epilepsy, Inc. Both organizations were young. The Epilepsy Foundation of Indiana started in 2006, the year after I graduated high school. The Angels4Epilepsy started in 2010, two years after my brain surgery.

It wasn't until 2009 that I was officially allowed to drive. I felt there was no stopping me now. So I contacted Jeff Rubenstein, the President of the Epilepsy Foundation of Indiana to see how I could be involved. We scheduled a meeting to personally meet one another and discuss some ideas. We talked about starting support groups and creating awareness. Probably my best memory from our meeting was Jeff's advice and guidance.

It was wonderful meeting with Jeff; it allowed me to learn more about the Epilepsy Foundation. Our meeting motivated and helped me understand that I'm not alone. It helped me to understand how I may reach out and help others. Jeff's advice was simple, yet heartfelt, and I will never forget his phrase, "spread the word" and create awareness. It finally all made sense. I found my calling and it's now our motto. We now have epilepsy support groups. I offered to start one in Anderson, Indiana. Jeff, my husband, and I ended up on the morning news sharing our story and where we came from.

The Epilepsy Foundation of Indiana is continuing to grow. We started the first support group in Anderson this year. The more we "Spread the Word" the more volunteers arrived dedicated, devoted, and determined to help. Then more and more support groups started to appear. Not too longer after volunteering for the Epilepsy Foundation of Indiana and starting a support group. I found a wonderful website, www.Angels4Epilepsy.org. This is a non-profit organization that started with a few volunteers with tremendous hearts. On the website a mother shared an amazing story of her seven year old daughter, Jamie. Jamie and I have a lot in common. She too has epilepsy. After struggling with testing, she spoke to her mom with motivation and determination. She wanted to start a non-profit organization to provide gift bags for children with epilepsy while they are in the hospital.

After reading her testimony, I couldn't help but cry. It was so moving and deeply touched my heart, because I have been there. I've spent many endless days in the hospital for testing. So frustrated, stressed, depressed, and it felt hopeless. On the website was an e-mail address so I had to contact them to share my story and how moving Jamie's testimony was. After speaking to Jamie's devoted mother, Judy, I felt my heart crying out wanting to help in any way I could. I contacted a well-known children's hospital in Indiana and requested a list of donation requirements. Then contact Judy to share their information. It seemed like a few days later, I received boxes and boxes of bags to share in Indiana. A wonderful friend of mine helped me sort the items and package the bags. After all was said and done, we ended up with 35 bags full of coloring books, crayons, book markers, puzzles, toys, Jamie's testimony, a seizure diary, and a bunch of information donated from the Epilepsy Foundation.

Now that I look back on my life it all makes since. My mother said as a child I was outgoing, motivated, and a leader. I always dreamed of being an elementary teacher and was and still teased for being a mother figure. I may have been shy during junior high and high school, but if there is one thing I have learned through my experience from battling with epilepsy, it was never be ashamed or afraid of being yourself. I live each day as if there is no tomorrow because I'm living proof that all dreams can come true.

Discovering Me

This incredible energy flows through me,

That makes me feel as if I'm free,

As I run through the meadows,

And swim through the sea,

I look at all that is great in life,

I'm finally happy being me,

No more pain to lock me away,

Only happiness shines through me now,

I've found my path to self-discovery.
By: Stacey Burns

Inspiration

Our motivation in life

Rewarding

~Ann Gillie

Karl J. Bos *from Canada*

I was born in May of 1979, and according to my family, my first sei-zure I ever had was 9 months later. It really frightened my mother, as she was a single parent with 2 boys, and the youngest boy having sei-zures. She never witnessed anyone having a seizure until her own son began having them, me. She brought me to the hospital not knowing what to do. The type of seizures I was having at that time was grand-mal seizures, which a lot of people are familiar with these days. She was going through so much hassle trying to explain to pediatricians and other doctors that she swears I was having epileptic seizures, but the doctors kept saying that she was wrong.

Some doctors thought I had ADHD, some just really had no idea. When I was 7 years old, the type of seizures I was having changed, so once again, my mother was explaining this to the doctors, and still would say she was wrong, but they were feeding me medica-tions used for epilepsy, and that totally changed the type of kid I was. Before taking any medications, I used to eat anything and everything, but when I was prescribed on to phenobarbital, I ate almost nothing, and all I did was wake up, have a seizure, and go back to bed. I slept about 18 – 20 hours a day.

There was an EEG that I had to do when I was in grade 3, where I had to stay awake for 24 hours before having the EEG. Boy was I ever tired. At the age of 10, I was introduced to a neurologist for the first time, and he was very understanding, very caring, and knew ex-actly what I was going through. My family and I all thought this was the best neurologist I had, and of course the medications I was on changed over and it helped for a short period of time, but then we be-gan to experiment on other kinds of mediations for epileptic seizures. He also asked me if I was willing to try brain surgery to possibly be-come seizure free. I was terrified of becoming mentally retarded, so I said no immediately, and never to ask again. After experimenting a bit, my neurologist was no longer a doctor.

We were then introduced to another neurologist, he decided to raise the medications a bit, and surprisingly, I was seizure free for approximately 8 months. I was very excited, and the next time we met up with the doctor, he told me to stop taking my pills, as it is not needed anymore. My mother asked if we should gradually lower the pills before taking him completely off, and the doctor disagreed with what my mother asked, so I stopped taking the pills immediately. 5 days later, what do you think started to happen? I was having 10 – 20 seizures in one day, and it was very frightening for me and my family. The next visit we had, that doctor denies telling me to stop taking my medications. Due to that mistake that doctor made, I did not want to see him ever again. I was then introduced to another neurologist that seemed knowledgeable, but had such a strong accent, where I could not understand 70% of the words he was saying. One thing I did understand him say was brain surgery. Again, I was too terrified and immediately told him no.

During this entire time, I was having about 5 – 15 seizures a month, and since the age of 7, I was having complex-partial seizures. I began to day-dream, as it would follow to me sleepwalking. Back in school, it was very embarrassing, because I would be made fun of from a lot of people in the school, and it made me mad inside, and for me being mad inside, what do you think would happen? Of course, I would have a seizure. Whenever I was overly angry, stressed, depressed, frustrated, excited, or lack of sleep, I would have a seizure. I was so waiting to finish school, so I would not have to be made fun of all the time. I was working very hard to feel like a regular student in school, and I told myself, I want a 70% or above for my overall average in high school. Seeing I am so hard on myself, I was grounding myself if my marks were below 70%, but would tell my friends, my mother grounded me.

Once I graduated from high school, I achieved a 70.6% average, and I was happy for myself in achieving my one goal I set for myself. Since I had the determination in me to succeed a 70% or above, and believed I could do it, it led me to achieving my goal. Since then I have been setting goals for myself each and every year. With many things in life, people say to me that they would never do anything like what I am doing, and one great example was that my part-time job that was giving me 100% coverage on my medical benefits, was located in Ajax, Ontario, and for one solid year, I was going to Mohawk College located in Hamilton, Ontario. With me not driving, I had to take public transit every Tuesday, & Friday from Hamilton to Ajax, and coming back home on the Wednesday, and Sunday, still working my 3 shifts a week, which was the first time I was living independently. My commute time was about 3.5 hours long in one direction. I was still never late for work, so people saw how determined I was.

After going to Mohawk College for a year, I was working 2 jobs. One job was working Wed-Sun 4pm - Midnight, and the grocery store working Thurs-Sun Midnight – 8:30 am. I did that for 4 months, as I was having so many seizures due to lack of sleep, and over working myself. I had to quit one of the jobs, so I kept the one job that was giving me my medical benefits. After a while, I was posting for a full-time position, and with my seniority, I ended up transferring to Scarborough, working full-time hours. My average commute was 1.5 hours long one-way. I got used to that commute and had no problem making that commute. Then this company began to transfer me throughout Toronto. With all the transfers I was given, I was fixing up so many stores, and they went against the union rules of transferring me a maximum of once every 6 month, and within 10km of my home store.

Well, I got transferred 13 times in 3 years, and I moved my home 3 times to get closer to work, just to see them transfer me again. When I was living in Mississauga, Ontario to be closer to work, they sent me downtown Toronto, and just after the Christmas season, they put me on long-term disability for some strange reason. I didn't understand why, and I was getting bored at home doing nothing. I was tempted to find another job, but if I did that, I would have been terminated, as I was claiming long-term disability, and working somewhere. So I waited 6 months to get back to work. I think the only thing that allowed me to return to work was me phoning them every week asking if I am returning to work next week, as that began to bother them.

At the last store I was at, I was on the day shift, and I had a seizure in front of a customer, which apparently complained to my manager about the services I was giving, as I had a seizure and she didn't real-ize that. I was then suspended for 5 days, which got me angry. I was so frustrated, seeing this is dealing with my epilepsy again. I marched out with anger, to the bus stop, and 2 days of me being at home on suspension, I got a phone call saying I am terminated. I got even more angry, and wanted to know the reasoning of termination, and they created a story saying I wrote down someone's license plate on my way out the door to the bus stop when I was told about my suspen-sion, so now I am a threat to the company and I am not allowed on premises for 6 months or I will be arrested.

At this time, my family was living in Ajax, ON, as I was living inde-pendently in Mississauga, ON. That was a financial crisis right there. During that time I was living in Mississauga, I found a neurologist that was right across the road from my home, asking my family doctor to refer me to this neurologist.

For the 3rd time, this neurologist asked me if I am willing to go through with brain surgery. I told him no, because I am afraid of becoming mentally retarded, so then he explained more about the process of brain surgery. He told me that I need to be tested first, because not all people with epilepsy are eligible for brain surgery, so why don't you just try the tested to see?

That was more comforting for me, and he gave me 2 options. He said we can use the hospital in Toronto, as they are somewhat new to the brain surgery process, or if you want someone with more experience, one of the Canada's best hospitals in London Ontario can help you. Which hospital would you prefer? I decided London. He then told me that a neurologist in London used to be his teacher, so there is a strong bond between these 2 neurologists.

At this time, I was in a financial crisis, as I got wrongfully dismissed from my work, and had no medical benefits any more. I was then of-fered to stay with my mother and her BF, and just pay a small amount for rent to help one another out. I was very thankful for that, and then found it easier to go through with brain surgery, as I do have home care, if I go through the process. I then found another job as a wrapper in a warehousing store in the bakery department, and one employee saw me have a seizure, and then they created a story about me saying something to someone, and the managers asked me "We know what you did, and have people here witness what you did, and it's up to you to reveal it and just quit, or for us to review everything and if you are wrong, you would be terminated, what is your choice?" I knew where this was leading, so I just quit, as they will find any reason to terminate me.

Again, I was given another job, at another retail store, and I felt bad that my 2nd Thursday at work, I had to book off, as I had my first appointment at the London Health Sciences Center. I was placed on another medication, and with me just starting this new job, and this new medication, I was extremely dizzy from the medication for 5 days straight, but still attended work, trying to hide my dizziness. I then called the doctor telling him I am going back to what my medications were before and we'll meet up again in a few months. This happened in September 2007. In December 2007, I had been given a call to come into the hospital to do my electrode testing. I booked off 6 working days just before Christmas to have my electrode testing done, and I had 4 seizures during that time, and they could not see exactly where the seizures were starting and ending.

The first seizure I had during the testing, the nurses in the epilepsy unit didn't even realize that my seizure was still occurring, a visitor of a patient beside me asked me if I noticed I just had a seizure, and I said yes, I just got out of it about 30 seconds ago, as the nurses thought it was done about 90 seconds ago. So, I got their attention and told them my seizure had just ended approximately a minute ago (by the time I got the nurses attention) as they thanked me for informing them that information, and know for the next seizure. I met quite a few new people who also have epilepsy, and there was one lady that just finished her brain surgery, and gave such a positive feedback about her surgery, and helped others, including me, with our self-esteem.

Due to not knowing exactly where the seizures were coming from, they had to do a Sub-Dural surgery which I agreed to do, and they explained to me that they would be drilling 2-4 holes in my skull, but I would be put asleep for this entire surgery. I accepted that, as we still did not know they answer about me being eligible for brain surgery.

On Saturday March 28th, 2008, I was put into the hospital to reserve the bed, as on Tuesday April 1st will be the day I have my sub-Dural surgery. Seeing I am a joker, especially on April Fool's Day, I asked the friendly nurses if they could do me one small favor after my surgery? I asked them if they could phone my mother at home, ask her to sit-down, relax and remain calm, and then just tell her that Karl says April Fools. They nurses laughed at it, but didn't want to help me with that, as they also expected me to forget for the first hour or so after this sub-Dural surgery.

This sub-Dural surgery took approximately 5 hours long, and the only thing I remember was being given a needle and I was asleep within 6 seconds. When I woke up at 7pm, I saw one of the nurses next to my bed, as she was going to bring me back to the epilepsy unit, and the first thing she said to me was "You mother is upstairs in the epilepsy unit" and I replied "Yeah, April Fools to you too". I still want you ladies to phone my mother with this joke. She seemed shocked I remembered that so fast.

Once we got to the epilepsy unit, my mother was not visible, so I asked them to call her, and then the joke came onto me, as my mother walked out of the bathroom. I did not expect anyone to come for a 3 hour drive just to see me for an hour or so, and to do another 3 hour drive back home. I thanked her allot right there.

I was in the hospital for about 3 weeks with my sub-Dural's connected to me, as I wanted to have my seizures, and as much as possible, so I felt if I over worked myself on the treadmill, it might help me have a seizure. It sure seemed to have helped, as I had 4 seizures, and all 4 seizures were exactly the same. They all started at the left temporal lobe and moved to the right. In the middle of April, I was then told that I am eligible for brain surgery, and the worst that can happen for me, with a 30% possibility is losing my short-term memory for 1 – 2 years, the other 70% chance of living seizure free, and lower than 1% chance of passing away.

Without me asking any of my friends, family, co-workers, etc, etc, I told myself immediately that I am going to do this brain surgery regardless of what anyone else thinks, because this is an open door for me. I must say, I currently don't like the room I am in and need to leave this room, and have the courage to walk through that slightly open door and enter the new room, and to make it a better room than I am in, in hopes of being seizure free in that new room.

As I got back to work, I had to catch up on a lot of the work that was saved for me, which I accomplished. And I know I was getting frustrated with many issue with my work again. I did not understand why my benefit package arrived 2 months late, and why it said I was only part-time. I was working constant full-time hours from day one. I then became full-time in December 2007, and my benefits kicked in then too. I did not get paid anything from those 6 days I took off, and same for the 3 weeks I just took off in April 2008, and my job title said "Sales Representative" as I was working as a "Receiver". When I contacted my law firm, they made a phone call to my home-office and store manager, and approximately 2 hours later, I got called into the office, as I was expected to be terminated again. Well, that did not happen.

They had me sit down, and they explained how they fixed everything, my requested wage, job title, short-term disability payments, and that I am full-time. I thanked them, but didn't believe it until I saw my next pay stub. I was given $2,700 for my back pay of everything they owed me; my job title changed to Receiver and was given my raise too. The next concern I had was when the official Receiver comes back from his long-term stress leave, what happens to me? I then heard of a store opening up in Whitby, Ontario (where I was living at the time) and was told I need to come for an interview at the job fair.

After my shift at work, I went to the interview of the job fair, and was told to meet up with the General Manager. When I had this interview, I explained to him that I was on a waiting list for brain surgery, and I could be off work for 3-6 months, in the near future, and his response to me was "Pretend you never told me that" I said ok, and proceeded with the interview. I then heard that there were 9 people wanting to transfer into this store, as only 2 of us got transferred, and I was one of the lucky candidates.

As I transferred store in August 2008, I met a lot of new people, and my general manager has made me a store lead, which really shocked me, and made me feel important. Seeing I already worked for this company for almost a full year, I knew most of the stuff I was doing. I helped with the store opening, as I did have experience in opening many stores in my past, as a temporary job. This was my 6th store I have helped open/close/renovate.

I began to train others how to read a plan gram, and explain about the sku numbers, etc etc. During the store opening, I was getting a little frustrated here and there, as my new General Manager wanted to know what was disturbing me. I apologized, and just let it go. He began to teach me more and more in life, and how to become more successful in life, as he knew my determination, and hard work, and being so brave to go for brain surgery. This store was very supportive of me and scared for me, as they told me they would give me their thoughts and prayers.

Of course, as I expected, people were asking me, "Don't you want to think or talk about it first? Aren't you scared to have this surgery?" As other's were terrified for me, I was brave enough to tell myself I am going to do this regardless of anyone's thoughts. My brother, my best friend, co-workers were all terrified for me, and was shocked I was not terrified. When they said they would give me their thoughts and prayers, it shocked me even more as I only expected about 4 people to care about me, but I heard from about 80 different people, people from work, my friends, my business partners, my mother's friends of friends, you name it, and they thought of me. I truly thank them all.

I had another appointment in London about a month before my surgery, with a speech-language pathologist, and she wanted to show me 30 difference pictures and see what I know, and test me before, during and after my surgery, to see where my memory lies at each time, as her goal was to make sure my memory is back to what it is before my surgery.

On Tuesday November 17th, 2008, I asked if I could take the afternoon off work, as I needed to get my Legal Will & Powers of Attorney completed, just in case I were to pass away from brain surgery, at least everything will go where I want it to go. On the way to the law firm with my mother, I received a phone call from London Health Sciences Center, saying that my surgery will be this Friday. Please register at 6:00am and surgery will begin around 8:00am. Immediately, I called my work and told them that I will not be into work as of Friday November 21st, 2008 for 3-6 months, as that is when my surgery is going to take place. They were all prepared for that, as I did train someone on the process of receiving.

On Thursday November 20th, I left work early to go down to London to stay at a Guest Home so I was there first thing the next morning. As I left my work, everyone was giving their heart to me and it felt so loving, and I thank them all for their support and care for me. My mother and I went to London, as she was already terrified for me, and she was shocked I wasn't scared. They only thing I was concerned about on the way to London, was the weather, as we heard on the radio there is 30 – 50 centimeters of expected snow in London.

We then arrived in London; the amount of snow on the ground didn't look any different than our home area, so we all thought they were wrong about the weather, but starting Thursday night in the overnight hours, that is when the heavy snow began. We arrived at the Guest Home, and they were so caring for us and thoughtful, and they even offered to shovel the driveway at 5am, just so we can leave at 5:30am, as we both told them to remain asleep, it's not needed. As we woke up, and looked out the window, the car was covered with about 15 centimeters of snow already, but it was light snow, so I wiped off the car, as my mother drove with fear, but also with courage and love for me.

We got to the hospital, and after my registration, my mother began to panic even more, and she asked me two questions that she said she would ask me again after surgery, to test what my memory level is at, as we were warned that for the first 24-48 hours, my short-term memory could be totally gone. What my mother wanted me to remember was the page she was on in her book and what date was.

As I got pulled away, my mother began to cry as she was so fearful of my surgery, and caring for her son. I felt that in my heart, but I also felt very brave to walk through this door to enter my new room. As I was put into the surgery room, I felt like I was entering that doorway now. I remained calm, as many people in the surgery room did not expect that. I told myself, that if I remain calm, and just let the surgeon do what he has to do, it won't interrupt him with his work, so just remain calm, and relax.

During my surgery, I asked my neurosurgeon when he was going to take pictures of my brain, as he previously told me to bring my own camera, and he will take a few pictures. He was shocked I remembered during surgery, and asked me where my camera was, and my exact answer was, "On the upper right part of my suitcase" as one of the assistants got the camera, and shocked everyone I remembered exactly where my camera was. He then took 3 pictures, 2 of my brain, and one picture of my face during my surgery.

After a while, I did get tired, so I felt asleep, and got woken up not long after to be tested. I was asked to count backwards from 20 over and over again. Once I messed up on my count, he knew not to take that part of my brain out, but if I counted back no problem, then it was a dead brain cell. They also tested me on the 30 pictures that I was tested a month before surgery, to see what my memory level was at. Overall, it was pretty good. I was told they took out the size of a fist out of my brain. My surgery lasted about 6.5 hours, as I was told it would take 8.5 hours long, but because I remained so calm, it made the surgery easier and faster for the neurosurgeon.

I was then placed into the emergency room, and after being there for a while, I heard my mother's voice in the hallway, and immediately told myself "I need to tell her what page she was on and today's date" The first second I saw her, I told her "Mother, you were on page 212, and today is Friday November 21st, 2008". She immediately began to cry, as she was so shocked to hear that from me. It was a great feeling in my heart. Later on that night, I was the shocked to see my mother's boyfriend show up at the hospital, as we are 3 hours away, and there is a terrible snow storm happening outside. He was terrified for the both of us, as I had surgery, and my mother may need support from someone if I was not successful.

On the Saturday, my mother's boyfriend had to go back home, but was thankful we were all doing well. My mother decided to stay until Monday, and then she will picked me up when it's time for me to leave. On that same day, I heard doctors saying they are trying to get me out of the emergency room, and place me somewhere else, as I am doing great. They couldn't find any other place, so I remained in the emergency room all day Saturday, and Sunday, and then on Monday, I had a few more check-up's with my memory, and my physical ability, as they knew I lived downstairs from my family, and wanted to see if I am able to walk up and down 9 individual steps. I decided to walk up a full flight of stairs which was 13 steps, and back down, and she said to me, do you realize you did more than 9, and I said yes.

I now told myself, I am in my new room, and out of that negative room, and I am going to make this the best room I was ever in and when I am fully recovered, I am going to help others living with epilepsy.

On Monday November 24th, 2008, I was then told I am going home today, so I got dressed, and my mother arrived around 1:00pm, and was going to leave to go home, and she asked where I was going, and I said I am going home, as she thought I was just changing rooms. I told her "No, I am going home with you" Now she thought I lost my memory, so she asked the doctor's and sure enough, they told her "Yes, Karl is good to go home now" as my mother burst into tears again.

As we were in the lobby waiting to get picked up from a driver at the Guest Home, my mother was willing to pay $40/night for the Guest Home, and so she thought it was an even $200, and I told her no, it total's $160. She again thought my memory is messed, so I told her to pay for Thursday night, Friday night, Saturday night, and Sunday night, as you are not staying Monday night, right? She was shocked at my memory and catching her mistakes. Once we got back to the Guest Home to pick up our stuff, we drove off, and I asked her "Did you pay them the $160.00?" As her response was "Oh crap, I forgot" At the same time, she got a phone call from her boyfriend, and she said she will call him back once we are on the highway. She then apologized for not giving anything as she just forgot. They were thankful for that, as we were thankful for them helping us. Once we got onto the highway, I asked her if she is going to call her boyfriend, and she was shocked I remembered that too, as she forgot that too. I was beginning to laugh at her memory loss, not mine.

During the drive home, it was ugly weather of wet-snow and I know my mother fears of driving in that weather, so I thanked her about 5 times on the way home, and she didn't expect me to say thanks that many times. About 5 hours later, we arrived into Whitby, and just before we were getting off the highway, I asked her not to drive on this one street because it was so bumpy and it will make my head hurt more. She didn't understand why she would have to go on that street, so I reminded her we need to go there for my medications of the pain killers. She was shocked I remembered again, as she forgot, AGAIN!

One week later, I had my 33 staples removed from my head from my family doctor, as he expected me to feel a bit of pain, but it was pretty fast for him to remove them. He was very proud for me to have the courage to do all this, and will have the will power. Once I arrived home, I felt bad that I was not able to shovel the driveway and sidewalk, as that is normally my responsibility. My mother attempted, but her Fibromyalgia caused her pain, and her boyfriend's heart caused him pain, so we had a neighbor that helped us out. Each day, I told myself to at least walk up the stairs, do something, and then walk down. Then I was asked by my best friend if I wanted to go for a walk in the mall, to get some of my exercise, as we can stop when I feel I have to, but I did one total distance of the mall about 4 times a week, and it really helped me recover faster and faster.

After my 6 week check-up, I asked if I was able to shovel the driveway, and I was told I can do whatever I want, but if I get dizzy or a headache, you must stop immediately. I then told myself, even if there is going to be a lot of snow, I will start the shoveling when the snow is only 1-3 centimeters high, and take a 3 hour break, and go back outside to continue shoveling, and I felt that helped me recovery faster and faster too. There was one day where I wasn't dizzy or given any headache, and saw 2 elderly couple shoveling their driveway, as I began later than them, and finished before them, so I felt I feel good enough to help them until I get dizzy or given a headache. I helped them quite a bit, as they wanted to pay me, and I said "No, this is from my heart for helping you, please keep that money" They both thanked me sincerely.

From that day on, I have been a very helpful person in so many ways. I was asked to do a presentation at a Gala in front of 220 people about my success of brain surgery, and going into newspapers, and on television. Once I heard a friend of mine who also had surgery for his epilepsy, he said I should go in newspapers, and on television, and so I made that a goal for me, and achieved that too. I also wanted to host a long bike ride to help fund raise and grow awareness for Epilepsy. On the 3rd weekend of August 2010, I rode my bike from Oshawa to Burlington along the Waterfront Trail and back, which totaled 280km distance in 2 days. I was very proud of myself to do that, and many people have been proud for me going so far.

At the same time, I have been helping others who have been thinking about brain surgery and wanted to know how I am doing and what I did in regards to my surgery. There was one couple from Ottawa, ON that the husband was thinking about brain surgery, and I had an appointment with my neurologist as he had his sub-Dural surgery, and met them in person. When I heard his surgery was Wednesday

February 3rd, 2010, I asked my supporting manager if I would take the Friday off work, as I want to take the bus down to London to support him and his family. The minute the patient woke up from his surgery, he began to cry to see me come all that way just for him. It felt good to fill my heart out for others. On the Sunday morning, when I had to leave, I then saw his wife cry, and I apologized for leaving, but I did have to work. They both were very thankful for me coming that far just to support them.

At the end of June 2009, I moved from Whitby to Ajax, (one town west) and just before I moved, I renewed my medications, and on the date of moving, when I began living in Ajax, was I able to find my medications? Scary enough to say, I did not find them for 3.5 weeks, and so I began taking the medications again, but was slowing increasing my medications to what it was supposed to be at. Then I began seeing my emotions and attitudes change in that negative direction again, so I gradually want back off my medications until I have a seizure. As I waited,

I was being cautious about me having a seizure, still with the belief of remaining seizure free. In December 2009, I had to be honest with my neurologist, and neurosurgeon that I have not been on any medications for about 4 months, and still no seizures. They were shocked on that information, but I had to be honest with them, and told them that if I had/have a seizure, I am putting myself liable for that, not any doctor. I wanted to make sure they had the right information about me in their records.

The following year, on November 29th, 2010, I had another follow-up appointment, as the just want to see how things are going, and I had a DVD, and 4 newspaper articles scattered across the desk, and he was shocked to see how successful I have been, and told me with his honesty, I was on the easier patients he has worked on, as I remained so calm, and recommended I share my success story with the London Health Science Foundation, which I have accomplished.

Today, I volunteer for so many organizations and feel proud of myself, and love how I am helping others. I help others if they have a legal situation with the legal membership I currently have, and for some, just giving them my feedback on my brain surgery, and it shocks me so much to hear so many people say to me that I am a true inspiration to them. Never in my lifetime have I expected to hear that.

As I have been getting more involved with Epilepsy organizations, I have been having fun in meeting new people and helping people. The first year I joined the event "Purple Day" in 2010, I went downtown Toronto and had a purple glow stick and we all went into the shape of a lavender ribbon, to help grow awareness for epilepsy. In 2011, I told myself I am going completely purple and I don't care if people think I look like an idiot, I want to help grow awareness.

On top of that, I have joined the Scotiabank Waterfront Marathon on behalf of Epilepsy Toronto, where I first ran 5km in 30 minutes and 46 seconds. The second year, I decided to walk, with the Epilepsy banner and wear my purple hat and wig. It was a good laugh for many, as I am now known as "The Purple Guy" lol

On top of all this I have been advertised in quite a lot of areas of media, and a few websites-

http://www.lhsf.ca/why-give/inspirational-moments/read-more-stories/karl-j-bos

http://www.newsdurhamregion.com/news/article/159523

One of my other goals was to have my life story authorized in a book that can be published, as I would love to help others and give my support in any ways possible. My contact e-mail is: epilepsy.awareness.on@gmail.com or kjbos.ppl@gmail.com

The way I look at life today is that I have the freedom, and I am thinking big as nothing is going to stop me to keep improving in life. I feel in my heart I can also help others that very same way. One quote I truly believe in is "If you mind can conceive it, and my heart can believe it, I know I can achieve it".

Sincerely, Karl J. Bos

Confidence

Is an inner assurance

Certainty

~Ann Gillie

Sarah Brown *from USA*

It's not the most beautiful story, but it was a miracle none the less. My seizures began at the age of three caused by encephalitis (inflammation of the brain). I would not have any reoccurring seizures until about the age of 10. From that point I battle clonic tonix seizures, the grand mals, until I reached early high school. In the beginning years of high school I started having clonic tonic seizures. Brain surgery was starting to be brought up at doctor appointments because medication was not treating my seizures.

At that time I was so scared of having surgery! I remember the first time they talked to me about it, I went in to the doctor appointment alone, wanting to be all grown up. I left in tears because nobody was going to take part of me away! It reminded me of a concentration camp and I couldn't escape! A few years later, after switching doctor's the idea of having brain surgery was brought up again. This time I handled it much better. Of course, I was also having 3-4 seizures a week and did not know it. I began college still seizing...... The worst part about having epilepsy is when you feel alone, when you get depressed. You feel like the entire world doesn't understand, doesn't care and you can't explain to them what's going on.

Since my seizures fired from my hippocampus I don't remember much from childhood to my first senior year of college. I do however remember crying all the time, asking God to take this burden away. I remember that my speech was effected pretty badly...finishing sentences in an actual flowing thought process never happened. Reading took my 2-3 times longer than other students, and math, forget it! I had brain surgery my senior year of college. My surgery took place at Cleveland Clinic Main Campus, Ohio. My surgery took place nearly 3 years ago and I have been seizure free for nearly 2 years.

After surgery I can look back and say, for me, it wasn't living with epilepsy that was the hardest part of life, it was living life afterwards. My coping with life wasn't as easy as other seizure patients because I had skipped so many development/social steps that it was hard to put together what life was like. Here, I had been living like a teen-ager all through my late teens early twenty's but had never developed mentally/ socially. The first difference I noticed after surgery was that I could read! I could read chapter after chapter and everything flowed. I took talk much faster without long pauses to find my thought process, I said whatever I was thinking, which got me into trouble a few times and I made it a personal goal of mine to tell others what it's like to live with a disability, and to be OK with who you are!

I graduated from Ball State University; IN I have a Bachelor's of Fine Arts degree in ceramic art. My work is inspired by living through epilepsy and overcoming it. I am now working to learn about other disabilities, creating art to tell stories about how, (we the people with disabilities live). Things that are happening that I thought I would never accomplish in my life, graduating from college, driving a car, owning a car, reading lots of reading, going to graduate school (art therapy), being a responsible adult!

Ann thanks for all you do!

Sarah Brown

Accomplish

To complete a task in life

Achieve

~Ann Gillie

Narelle from *Australia*

My name is Narelle, I was born on the 2nd March 1973 perfectly normal until I was 3 months old when I had a reaction to a needle called triple antigen for measles mumps and rubella left me with cerebral palsy (right side hemiplegic) which means I am paralyzed down the right side of my body.

The doctors told my parents I would not walk, talk, or do anything for myself and when I had the reaction it also split my brain in half, I can't do math or money because that part of the brain is not there, it is just a big white mass and I function on half a brain.

I was having 6 or 7 seizures a day, 2 or 3 during the night and on 37 tablets a day until I went into hospital on the 15th of August 1997 and had 3 weeks of electrodes in my head seeing where the seizures were coming from. Luckily they were able to get it in the right spot to be able to take the part of the scar tissue out of my brain that the seizures were coming from, I had the operation on the 25th August 1997 had 6 mini seizures after the surgery and have been seizure free since.

I now live on my own in my own unit and also have my driver's license it has really changed my life and it was the best thing I ever did!

Narelle

Narelle's story hits home with me in that I to was paralyzed when I was younger and it was my right side as well. My parents were also told I would not walk, would have speech problems, probably not be right handed; the list of things I was not supposed to do went on and on. Well I kicked ass when it came to showing those doctors; I am right handed, walk, talk and like I have said before, am on top of the world!

Ann

Positive

An incentive to grow

Affirmative

~Ann Gillie

Dana Leahy Janssen *from USA*

"It's not like it was BRAIN SURGERY or anything - wait, yes it was!"

Today I am celebrating the second anniversary of my Temporal Lobectomy. What's that, you ask, and why in the world would I do such a thing?! Long story and most of you know it. But for those that don't, here goes:

Where do I begin? Let's see, it was the summer of 2007 just before the school year started; Patrick was going into the first grade, and Joe was in pre-school. Everything in life was moving along pretty well. I was all geared up to be one of those super-involved school moms; you know, the type that goes to every classroom party, and helps out with the spelling tests every week. But my brain had other plans for that year...

On Labor Day, somewhere around 3am, my husband David awoke to find me convulsing. He thought I was having a nightmare, and tried to wake me, but with no luck. Mind you, I have ZERO memory of this night; it's only how I've been told it happened. At some point, I got out of bed, and wandered downstairs. I tried to get into our office, but the door was locked, and I started to cry.

Of course, David was quite concerned with my strange behavior, and ran to get the phone to call his sister. He told her to come over immediately to watch the boys so he could take me to the hospital. He had been worried about me all weekend; I'd been acting "odd" and we would soon find out why. Anyway, by the time he came back, I was on the floor having what we now know was a full-blown grand-mal seizure; my arms were sticking straight out in the air, I was convulsing and foaming at the mouth. He dialed 911 immediately. Diann arrived just as the ambulance took us away to McPherson Hospital in Howell. They tried everything they could, but soon realized I needed to go to a bigger hospital with more resources.

They flew me in a helicopter to St. Joe's in Ann Arbor, and I was admitted. The last memory I have before the seizure was brushing my teeth on Sunday night. Everything after that is a big blank until two days later in the hospital. Most of my family was around me and I had no idea where I was or why. They all had to explain it to me repeatedly; about every twenty minutes. Think of the movie "Groundhog Day". I guess if it wasn't so scary, it would have been kind of funny?

The diagnosis went from tumors, to perhaps epilepsy, and back again. My MRI did show a mass on my brain was it a tumor? Could it be cancerous? The doctors were disagreeing on whether to proceed with a biopsy or not. That was a little upsetting to my husband, and he wanted a second opinion before agreeing to let them cut my head open! The neurologist on my case actually said this to him: "Well, if you want to get a second opinion from 'Joe-Expert' that's your right".

Anyone who knows David at all must be laughing at how much THAT did not go over so well with him. Thankfully, another doctor on my case took him aside later and said that if we really wanted a second opinion, she knew just the guy for the job...and he was at the University of Michigan.

Within a few days, I was home, and on some pretty intense anti-seizure medication. David had already been in contact with the recommended neurosurgeon, who scheduled me for a second MRI, and referred me to new neurologist. Right away, they diagnosed me with temporal lobe epilepsy, caused by mesial temporal sclerosis (scar-tissue in the middle part of my temporal lobe). Google those words if you want to know more! But apparently, it's fairly common, and it's the most common form of epilepsy for adults who have no childhood history of seizures.

I did a little research on my own too, and after discussing what I found with my doctors, I learned I'd been having seizures for at least ten years...but I just didn't know it! There are many different kinds, and I was having simple partial and complex partial seizures. Neither of which anyone could tell I was having by looking at me.

The simple partials are also known as "auras" or warning seizures, and many times precede the complex partials. They are so incredibly difficult to explain, and it sounds ridiculous...but they feel like having "deja vous". But not in a simple "hmmm, I remember this happening before", but an actual physiological wave of feeling would come over me, sometimes accompanied by nausea and a odd taste in my mouth. Never painful, just disturbing. I could never figure out what that sensation was, and it never occurred to me to mention it to my doctor. It often seemed triggered by something I saw on television. Was I remembering a dream? Did I have low blood sugar?

Maybe I'm psychic??!

The complex partials, we discovered, explained away all the years of thinking that I was hard of hearing. Countless times I had people tell me they were calling my name, but I didn't answer. Out of the blue, people would ask me in a panicky way, "Are you alright?? You look pale like you're about to pass out! I was talking to you for two whole minutes, didn't you hear me??!" I would get annoyed, thinking that they were full of crap, because I didn't hear a THING.

Well when you have a complex partial seizure, you lose consciousness for a few moments; anywhere from thirty seconds to two minutes. Therefore, it's not a good idea to drive a car if you have them. Which brings us to the topic of driving? Since I'd had a seizure, I was not allowed to drive. Each state has its own rules, and in Michigan, it's no driving for six months after having had a seizure. If you have another one, you start counting again! Doctors in Michigan are not required to report seizures to the state, and in my case it was left to my family to make sure I didn't drive. And boy, did they ever take care of that!

So, while I never legally had my license taken away from me, I may as well have. Not complaining at all, don't misunderstand me; they all swooped in and made sure my boys were taken to school every day, took me grocery shopping, EVERYTHING. My Mom practically lived with us for that time. I will be forever grateful to everyone who helped me. Friends, family, neighbors, everyone!

But it wasn't easy for me to lose control like that. Not to mention the fact that nobody left me alone for more than ten minutes during those first few months. It took one of my doctors to tell them they really didn't need to hover over me quite so much. I think he even said "you don't need to infantilize her". The day they finally dropped me off to meet some girlfriends at Starbucks, and walk around Target by myself for an hour was a glorious day. Even that little bit of freedom was such an amazing thing...

After being diagnosed, I was told that I was not likely to benefit from anti-seizure medication forever. I may not have grand-mal seizures, but the complex ones could continue (and they did), they would build up more scar-tissue in my brain, which would lead to more seizures, and so on...and then possibly another grand-mal. But surgery was known to be highly successful, and that was my best option. It would involve having the area around the scar-tissue removed. The front-half of my right temporal lobe, to be exact. Scary, right? But I could not imagine living for the rest of my life always being afraid of having another seizure, and not being allowed to drive for six months at a time. THAT was scary as hell. But brain surgery? Heck, why not? Bring it on!

I would have jumped on the operating table the very next day, if only they would have let me! Alas, good doctors don't just cut your head open and mess around in your brain on a whim. At least, not at the U of M. They started me on a series of tests, to make sure that I was a good candidate for the surgery; that not only would I stop having seizures, but that I would be able to walk, talk and remember things. You know the important stuff!

The first test was long-term EEG monitoring: in layman's terms, they put those little things on my head, wrap it all up in gauze (damn, I wish I had taken pictures) hook 'em up to a machine and wait for a seizure to happen. They had to lower my medication to assist with the process, and THAT was kind of scary. The hope was that I would have a few complex partials and they could determine if they were coming from my temporal lobe only. Why bother taking out half of my temporal lobe, if I was also having seizures that initiated from another part of my brain, right?

The hospital staff was on hand to monitor me and make sure I wouldn't have a BIG seizure, but I also had to have a family member stay with me...someone to be by my side to notice if I was "spacing out" and unresponsive. They would take note of the time, and any odd behavior I might exhibit, and the epileptologist would match that against the monitors. I was on video, too.

It took three days to have a seizure. And I had two "beautiful" ones, according to the neuro staff. As was suspected, they were coming only from my right temporal lobe. In the end, it turned out to be a fun bonding time with my Mom, who was the chosen one to stay with me. We watched TV, read magazines, and I became addicted to Sudoku. Did I mention this took place over Thanksgiving? Not the best turkey dinner I ever had, but it wasn't horrible, either. One test down, many more to go! I had some fairly in-depth speech and neuropsychological tests. You know, put the round peg in the round hole and the square peg in the square hole, all while wearing a blind-fold and using only one hand. Memory quizzes, and math, too...it was actually kind of fun, despite being four hours long.

The only invasive test I was given was the Wada test. You can Google that too...but I'll try to explain. The idea of it is fascinating, and the test itself was kind of a cool experience; what I can remember of it, anyway. But the path to get there was NOT FUN! Catheter in the groin, going up to my brain, by which they administered medicine to put half of my brain "asleep". This was to determine that when they turned my right side "off", would my left side be able to "pick up the slack", especially with my short term memory? I was shown a series of flash cards, and small household objects. Then they "turned off" the right half of my brain. I was shown the same pictures and objects again, along with some new ones, and was asked "Did you see this one before? This one?" and so on...

Apparently I did quite well, and my left side was able to recall every-thing it needed to. One very odd thing that I experienced: one of the pictures was of a hippopotamus. When I was shown that picture the second time around, I KNEW it was a hippopotamus, and I remem-bered that I had seen it earlier. But for just a little bit, I was having difficulty. My brain didn't want to deliver the word to my mouth, you know? I will never forget that odd sensation. It was like one of those dreams where you try to scream, but it just won't come out.

As uncomfortable and scary as some of the testing process was, it was all necessary to ensure I would have a successful outcome with my surgery. Every little bit helped me to feel secure, and that I was doing the right thing. And all along, it was my choice; no one ever told me I HAD to do it. Just that if I didn't, I was likely not to have success with medication only. And the medication has its own side-effects that I knew I didn't want to live with...but that's another long story.

In March, we got the phone call from my neurologist with the good news. And obviously, it wasn't a quick decision, either. See, after completing all of the tests, a committee of everyone that had seen me (and believe me, it was A LOT!) got together and went over my case and my results, and together they determined that I was indeed a good candidate for the surgery. I was a "textbook" case, it seems. Wednesday, April 16, 2008 would be the big day.

There is so much more I could describe about that day, and the months following, but this note is getting pretty long now. Most of all, just I wanted to share how my life was changed in an instant that Labor Day morning...and as scary as it was, and as difficult to deal with (I didn't even touch on the memory issues due to the seizures, or the depression and mood swings) I will be forever grateful that it happened the way that it did. My husband was home at the time; my boys were asleep and didn't see anything. Everybody was in the right place, at the right time, and I found the perfect doctors to solve my problem. It could have been much, much, worse.

Again, it wasn't easy...not by a long shot, but I feel so much better now, and more "myself" than I've ever felt in my life. Getting rid of the seizures has allowed the real me to come out. I was hiding in there somewhere, and now I've been given the permission to be ME! Mind you, not everyone in my inner circle has had an easy time with that...and the journey isn't over yet, either. The incredible amount of support and friendship I have gained over the past two and a half years is more than I ever could have asked for, and I thank ALL of you for that. No matter how small it may seem, every single one of you has made a positive impact in my life, and I love you for it. If you made it all the way through this note, I thank you for indulging me. And if you have any further questions, please don't hesitate to ask. Really, I love to talk about it. I am an open book! :)

As well as Dana I to was diagnosed with mesial temporal sclerosis! Ann

Journey

One step at a time

Unpredictable

~Ann Gillie

Helen Western *from UK*

Helen wanted to share her story with us in a poem!

A New beginning

Trapped in a world of physical restrain,
That world of dominance, that derelict domain
Of hopeless, helpless , pitiless pain
An end to the fear, dashed again
Yet through the turmoil, lay that thought
A cure, so dormant, will it ever be sought
Over the years the thought became real
An invaluable hand that could help and heal
My conscience stirred and before my eyes
Lay a brand new world, gone was the 'guise
The world was my oyster, that ray of hope, a gleam
As I realized a cure, was no longer a dream

"Ann you express an understanding that is imperative to the recognition and development of the world of epilepsy, its prevention and its cures. Thank you so much for your efforts"

Helen

Hope

Always a possibility

Potential

~Ann Gillie

Paul Elliott *from USA*

On the evening of Dec 6th 1972 I was in a motorcycle accident while attending aircraft maintenance school and taking flying lessons.. Injuries sustained in the accident were; traumatic brain injury, multiple compound fractures on my left leg and left arm. I also sustained third degree burns on my left lower leg. I have no memory of approximately the first 30 days following the accident. To date I have had fourteen surgical procedures performed as a result of that accident.

My first grand mal seizure occurred in 1986. The 2nd Grand Mal occurred within a week of the first one. After the 2nd grand mal I was put on Tegretol. From 1986 to February 2003 I took 2000 mg of Tegretol daily. When I was in the epilepsy monitoring unit at Barrows Neurological in 2003 it took over two weeks before I had a seizure. The first seizure put a rib out of joint from the severity of the muscle contractions. Grand mal seizures always left me unable to turn my head for several weeks and very sore from the muscle contractions.

Around 1988 the neurologist I was seeing asked me if I would consider surgery. My response to him was that I had had many surgeries on different areas but I always considered my head to be off limits. I finally came to the realization in 2002 that if I wanted to gain relief from 10 to 15 partial complex seizures a day that I needed to have surgery performed.

In 2002 the decision was made to proceed with the necessary evaluations at Barrows Neurological to be considered a surgical candidate. I remember when I had the depth wires installed at the EMU in Barrows I was told that epilepsy from a traumatic brain injury usually was due to a damaged hippocampus. The test in the EMU resulted in the entire hippocampus being removed on November 10th 2003. Unfortunately within a few months I started having partial complex seizures again. The frequency decreased considerably, however I was still having seizures. By April of 2004 we had decided to go ahead and remove the amygdala from the right temporal lobe. The months between April 2004 and February 2005 were the longest months of my life. I had already been through neurological surgery once and I knew the trials and torment involved with that surgery and I had to do it all over again.

The procedure to remove the amygdala was scheduled for February 14th 2005. That was the first available surgery date after a trade show that I attended every year. Following the first surgery in 2003 I developed an infection in a location above my right ear where a hollow bolt was located for one of the depth wires. I'm told that I was white as a ghost from the infection, was taken up to surgery and came down looking completely different. I have no memory of that surgery being performed. There is one hospital room I'm told I spent a few days in. However I don't have any memory of that room.

Following orthopedic surgery I've always been able to regain strength and movement through physical therapy and exercising. Following neurosurgery there aren't any therapy exercises to do to regain functions that were affected by the surgery. My epilepsy journey ended in October 2006 when I took my last Tegretol pill. One concern of my family members when I was coming off the Tegretol was about my decision to stop all medicine. Having gone through four surgical procedures I had decided to go for broke and become 100% medicine free. In all the years when I was taking the Tegretol when someone would ask me how I was doing my answer would often be, "It feels like I'm flying straight and level in for and haze. Now when someone asks how I am doing I reply, the sun is shining bright and I'm ready to fly acrobatic.

Optimistic

An encouraging feeling

Triumph

~Ann Gillie

CHAPTER 5

Questions And Answers

Meds? Surgeries? Side effects?

I was curious to see how many different answers I would get for these questions, but I was even more curious to how many answers would be the same. So these were the responses I got:

(I do include my own answers in here as well)

MY QUESTIONS

- **How many different meds have you been on for your seizures?**

- **Did epilepsy affect your education; either elementary, high school or college/university?**

- **Did or does having epilepsy affect any specific relationships in your life?**

- **Have you ever gone for a second opinion?**

- **Do you have any family members with epilepsy?**

- **Where is the most bizarre place you had a seizure?**

- **What were some of the side effects you encountered with your meds?**

- What was the name of your surgery?

- Since your surgery are you 100% seizure free?

- Do you ever regret having surgery?

- Who has been one of the most positive inspirations to you or in your life?

These are the answers which I received from people all over the world!

John from Australia

How many different meds have you been on for your seizures?

Answer: About 3 or 4

Did epilepsy affect your education, either elementary, high school or college/university?

Answer: I had a hard time concentrating for the most part, but other than that no!

Did or does having epilepsy affect any specific relationships in your life?

Answer: Not really

Have you ever gone for a second opinion?

Answer: No I didn't need to I had a great doctor

Do you have any family members with epilepsy?

Answer: nope

Where is the most bizarre place you had a seizure?

Answer: Probably in a restaurant

What were some of the side effects you encountered with your meds?

Answer: Dizziness and tired allot

What was the name of your surgery?

Answer: Right Temporal Lobectomy

Since your surgery are you 100% seizure free?

Answer: YES I am!!!

Do you ever regret having surgery?

Answer: NO WAY!

Who has been one of the most positive inspirations to you or in your life?

Answer: My parents

Ann (ME) from Canada

How many different meds have you been on for your seizures?

Answer: I was on about 5 or 6 different ones, the very first one being Phenobarb

Did epilepsy affect your education, either elementary, high school or college/university?

Answer: Yes I think it did, I made it through all…elementary, high school and college, but I definitely struggled, BUT did make it!!

Did or does having epilepsy affect any specific relationships in your life?

Answer: I think it did to a point, I sure relied on others allot, which now it is a great feeling to not have to anymore! I am my own person now and so very proud of that.

Have you ever gone for a second opinion?

Answer: YES and it was the best decision I have ever made in my life!

Do you have any family members with epilepsy?

Answer: None that I know of!

Where is the most bizarre place you had a seizure?

Answer: I had them in so many different places, but I would say the dentist and hairdresser!

What were some of the side effects you encountered with your meds?

Answer: Weight loss and weight gain, depression and dizziness

What was the name of your surgery?

Answer: Left Selective Amygdalohippocampectomy

Since your surgery are you 100% seizure free?

Answer: I am 110% seizure free!!!!

Do you ever regret having surgery?

Answer: That is one thing I will NEVER regret!!

Who has been one of the most positive inspirations to you or in your life?

Answer: My family and friends…but my Grampy was a huge one…I know he is still looking out for me!!

Stacey from USA

How many different meds have you been on for your seizures?

Answer: Too many to count 8 or 9

Did epilepsy affect your education, either elementary, high school or college/university?

Answer: yes all 3

Did or does having epilepsy affect any specific relationships in your life?

Answer: No

Have you ever gone for a second opinion?

Answer: No

Do you have any family members with epilepsy?

Answer: No

Where is the most bizarre place you had a seizure?

Answer: Walking home from school

What were some of the side effects you encountered with your meds?

Answer: dizziness room spinning rashes breaking out in hives

What was the name of your surgery?

Answer: Tiperlobactamy

Since your surgery are you 100% seizure free?

Answer: YES

Do you ever regret having surgery?

Answer: NO

Who has been one of the most positive inspirations to you or in your life?

Answer: ooooh that is a hard one, probably my family!

Jeanne from USA

How many different meds have you been on for your seizures?

Answer: I've been on too many meds to count, and many, many different combinations

Did epilepsy affect your education, either elementary, high school or college/university?

Answer: school through middle school was hard being made fun of

Did or does having epilepsy affect any specific relationships in your life?

Answer: I've been homebound due to epilepsy...since learning to drive I am never home

Have you ever gone for a second opinion?

Answer: Been to many Dr's

Do you have any family members with epilepsy?

Answer: my mother & her family going back 5 generations

Where is the most bizarre place you had a seizure?

Answer: I don't know

What were some of the side effects you encountered with your meds?

Answer: Blurred vision, feeling of paranoia on topamax, dizziness, being tired, shaky

What was the name of your surgery?

Answer: Right Temporal Lobectomy

Since your surgery are you 100% seizure free?

Answer: NO

Who has been one of the most positive inspirations to you or in your life?

Answer: Dad

Alison from USA

How many different meds have you been on for your seizures?

Answer: 4

Did epilepsy affect your education, either elementary, high school or college/university?

Answer: No

Did or does having epilepsy affect any specific relationships in your life?

Answer: No

Have you ever gone for a second opinion?

Answer: No

Do you have any family members with epilepsy?

Answer: No

Where is the most bizarre place you had a seizure?

Answer: I don't remember

What were some of the side effects you encountered with your meds?

Answer: Dilantin made my gums grow

What was the name of your surgery?

Answer: Right Temporal Lobectomy

Since your surgery are you 100% seizure free?

Answer: Yes

Do you ever regret having surgery?

Answer: No

Who has been one of the most positive inspirations to you or in your life?

Answer: My family

Beth from UK

How many different meds have you been on for your seizures?

Answer: two meds

Did epilepsy affect your education, either elementary, high school or college/university?

Answer: No

Did or does having epilepsy affect any specific relationships in your life?

Answer: Yes

Have you ever gone for a second opinion?

Answer: No

Do you have any family members with epilepsy?

Answer: No

Where is the most bizarre place you had a seizure?

Answer: I don't know

What were some of the side effects you encountered with your meds?

Answer: Anxiety, blurred vision, most of the other side effects faded

What was the name of your surgery?

Answer: Right Anterior Temporal Lobectomy

Since your surgery are you 100% seizure free?

Answer: Yes

Do you ever regret having surgery?

Answer: No

Who has been one of the most positive inspirations to you or in your life?

Answer: Family and Friends

Helen *from UK*

How many different meds have you been on for your seizures?

Answer: When my epilepsy started, the 'guinea pig' stages took me through four different types of medication, to find the right one for me.

Did epilepsy affect your education, either elementary, high school or college/university?

Answer: Before my epilepsy started, brain damage lay dormant and undiscovered. As time passed, the damage stirred but I remained determined. I passed my 11 plus, got to Grammar school, then my concentration became severely affected. I kept going and kept believing in myself and the future. I was a bit wobbly at school but stood firm and got all my qualifications at college. I then became a manageress at 21. Then epilepsy hit me hard.

Did or does having epilepsy affect any specific relationships in your life?

Answer: During grand mal seizures, parts of my body became damaged; my right arm suffered several severe dislocations that resulted in 5 operations. Muscles were tightened around the joint until a block was eventually put in. My partner at the time stopped me from choking once or twice but it didn't split us up. **It strengthened us.**

Have you ever gone for a second opinion?

Answer: I studied medicine for many years and realized that the temporal lobe area and the medication type and dosage were to be questioned. I also realized that certain characteristics I displayed were typical of damage to the temporal lobe. The professor was having none of it until I really put my foot down and asked for a second opinion. MRI scans were not displaying evidence of damage at the time, but limits to MRI's were not taken into account. I realized that I would benefit from invasive surgery, so put this to him. He slammed his hands on the desk and shouted 'there is nothing wrong with your brain!!!!!!!!!!!!!!!!!!!' then he said 'right that's it, you don't believe me, and I'm discharging you to the surgical team.'

Next thing I was having my head drilled while I was awake. I'll never forget that wide, loving smile of the doctor who had hold of my hand. The electrodes were placed onto the brain and meds reduced. Several severe seizures followed and were recorded.

Following this, I requested an 'Angio Wada' (memory) test, and was told they were only done under certain circumstances. I submitted my circumstances in the form of a case study, and got the test! During the test, it took 4 attempts to insert the correct sized tube into the femoral artery….blood everywhere. The place was packed, as the test was quite rare in the UK and during it, a student doctor collapsed. She was dragged out, mid-test. After the test, I was told 'ok you've passed'.

Eventually after many requests, studies, suggestions and consultations, initiated by myself, surgery ensued. A Mr. Eldridge waved the magic wand and removed the right temporal lobe.

I awoke into a new world. My seizures stopped. Two weeks later, I was called back to be told they had found brain damage. I was right. If I hadn't studied so much for so many years, I never could have put my case forward and wouldn't have had a case to press for the surgical team. I never would have been cured.

Do you have any family members with epilepsy?

Answer: No other members of my family had epilepsy or brain damage

Where is the most bizarre place you had a seizure?

Answer: The strangest place I had a seizure was sat in as a life model, in front of a handful of artists! It was a partial seizure but it didn't stop me. I saw the funny side. My manager at the time spotted it and diverted the artists' attention while I had the seizure.

What were some of the side effects you encountered with your meds?

Answer: tiredness, nausea, depression

What was the name of your surgery?

Answer: Right Temporal Lobectomy

Since your surgery are you 100% seizure free?

Answer: 110% seizure-free

Do you ever regret having surgery?

Answer: Absolutely no regrets

Who has been one of the most positive inspirations to you or in your life?

Answer: My influences are true 'enablers'. Those who take Joe Bloggs from MacDonald's and give them great success, not just a glimmer of hope.

Ashley from USA

How many different meds have you been on for your seizures?

Answer: I can say I have been on 10 different meds

Did epilepsy affect your education, either elementary, high school or college/university?

Answer: Yes Epilepsy effected my education. Made a slow learner and fail a few classes since I wasn't fast as others.

Did or does having epilepsy affect any specific relationships in your life?

Answer: It has affected my family most relationships I have been in. I guess they never understood Epilepsy unless they had it or been through it.

Have you ever gone for a second opinion?

Answer: I have gone for second opinions and each person said something different. So I followed what I thought was best. Starting with changing meds, VNS to Brain surgery.

Do you have any family members with epilepsy?

Answer: No one in my family has epilepsy

Where is the most bizarre place you had a seizure?

Answer: Most bizarre place if I had to think was school. So embarrassing and got picked on cause nobody understood it.

What were some of the side effects you encountered with your meds?

Answer: Side effects on meds I have had was overdose, Very tired, constipation or urinary tracts, hard to concentrate, made me feel slow

What was the name of your surgery?

Answer: Left temporal lobectomy

Since your surgery are you 100% seizure free?

Answer: So far I have been seizure free for 3 years and still going forward

Do you ever regret having surgery?

Answer: I don't regret having surgery at all. I wanted to do whatever it took to change my life and be seizure free. It took surgery. I will never regret it at all. It was the best thing I have ever done.

Who has been one of the most positive inspirations to you or in your life?

Answer: Inspirations in my life has been my family, allot of wonderful great friends that have stuck by my side, and God.

Mark from USA

How many different meds have you been on for your seizures?

Answer: 17

Did epilepsy affect your education; either elementary, high school or college/university?

Answer: Yes but learned to adjust

Did or does having epilepsy affect any specific relationships in your life?

Answer: Cousin on father's side

Have you ever gone for a second opinion?

Answer: YES

Do you have any family members with epilepsy?

Answer: NO

Where is the most bizarre place you had a seizure?

Answer: bottom of a whirlpool was 12 days in critical care.

What were some of the side effects you encountered with your meds?

Answer: lethargy

What was the name of your surgery?

Answer: Temporal lobe resection with hippocampus and amygdala

Since your surgery are you 100% seizure free?

Answer: YES

Do you ever regret having surgery?

Answer: NEVER

Who has been one of the most positive inspirations to you or in your life?

Answer: I hate to sound vein but myself now.

Sean from Scotland

How many different meds have you been on for your seizures?

Answer: about four or five

Did epilepsy affect your education, either elementary, high school or college/university?

Answer: Yes, I had a hard time concentrating and sitting still in class.

Did or does having epilepsy affect any specific relationships in your life?

Answer: Yes, some family members didn't handle my seizures very well, they almost seemed embarrassed, but my true friends were great.

Have you ever gone for a second opinion?

Answer: yes

Do you have any family members with epilepsy?

Answer: No

Where is the most bizarre place you had a seizure?

Answer: to be honest, the toilet, sorry if that is gross, but that's life.

What were some of the side effects you encountered with your meds?

Answer: depression and weight gain

What was the name of your surgery?

Answer: Right Temporal Lobectomy

Since your surgery are you 100% seizure free?

Answer: Yes and it is awesome!!

Do you ever regret having surgery?

Answer: No, why would I?

Who has been one of the most positive inspirations to you or in your life?

Answer: My friends!

_____

Thanks to all of you for sharing such personal answers with all of us on your experiences; some answers were very simple and to the point and others really decided to share their inner most feelings in their answers, which is awesome. I think after reading through the answers each one submitted it would be a safe assumption to say that all of us have **NO** regrets when it comes to having our surgeries.

We definitely went through some tough struggles and side affects but we are all now in a different place in our lives and would not be here if we didn't have our surgeries. I found some answers very interesting in that they were so very similar with the others, it appears that other than the **no regrets,** there was no immediate family history of epilepsy, the side effects from meds were almost exact, dizziness, depression, nausea; we should all be very proud of ourselves and remember we are on a roll and don't plan on slowing down anytime soon. This is our time, your time, and everyone's time to shine!

I applaud all of you for taking the time to be part of this book with me. Only a few of us have actually met one another but to me were are a newly formed family of friends!

CHAPTER 6

Women And Epilepsy

Women and epilepsy, that there is a topic that could snowball into allot of different conversations. I could refer back to Sex and Seizures, which I wrote about in my first book, or I could talk about menstrual cycles and seizures, being a mother with seizures, the topics are never ending. So I figured lets touch on some basics and go from there.

We all know women can be very different from men, no let's rephrase that, **WE ARE DIFFERENT THAN MEN**. So even when it comes to epilepsy women can be effected in different ways. The differences arise because of the common reason, that of our biological differences. Fertility rates for women that have epilepsy are about a third lower than the general population, this could be partly due to the fact that women with seizure disorders may be reluctant to get pregnant, and research has shown that these women face more menstrual abnormalities, polycystic ovarian syndrome and other reproductive problems which can interfere with their normal fertility. The causes of these reproductive problems have been linked to the side effects of certain anti-epileptic drugs (AEDs) and seizures.

It has been found to that some AED's can interfere with birth control pills, these meds are ones like Dilantin, Tegretol,(carbamazepine) and barbiturates such as Phenobarb, Prominal, Mysoline, and Topamax. I myself was on several of those, both Topamax and Tegretol, which I managed to have two healthy pregnancies with while on them both at the same time. I was on Phenobarb as a child, but that was a long, long time ago, ages ago!

Weight Gain and AED's

Some women do experience weight gain while taking certain AED's but they should understand that excessive weight can lead to other health risks such as:

- high blood pressure, heart disease, diabetes, and cancer

It is unfortunate that allot of women who gain weight on seizure medications decide to stop medication, which only causes more episodes of seizures. I did gain weight over the years of being on different epilepsy meds and it was extremely frustrating, I hated it; but I realized that weight gain was better than grand mal seizures or risking my life over. It is hard though to accept things like gaining weight, it just doesn't seem fair.

Seizures and Hormones

Our hormones play a significant role in the occurrence of seizures; for example, the severity and frequency of seizures often can change during puberty, during our monthly menstrual cycles, during pregnancy, and menopause. An astonishing 30% to 50% of women with epilepsy experience menstrual cycle-related seizures. I am one to vouch for that, as I would have more seizures during my period, it was awful. Here is me having severe cramps, the worst periods ever and a seizure on top of it all. I was a miserable person during these times, not someone you wanted to be around.

Some potential risks for women with epilepsy -

Increased risk of conceiving children born with birth defects – *I personally was on full medications with my first two pregnancies and had NO problems at all!*

Unwanted changes in body and facial hair – *I will say that for me I did gain weight, my hair turned grey – oh right I can blame that on boys and a husband!*

Obesity

Irregular periods and absent menstruation – *My periods were definitely off the wall, I would go only a couple weeks between periods and an actual period for me could last from 5 – 11 days.*

Can epilepsy affect my sex life?

Now there is a loaded question! I must say that epilepsy definitely affected my sex life and to be totally honest it wasn't for the good. I never worried though that I would have a seizure during sex; it never crossed my mind till years after my surgery when I spoke at a Sex and Seizures Forum in Edmonton, Alberta. There are some anti-epileptic drugs out there that can cause some women to have less interest in sex; and some peoples seizures might affect the way that their body releases hormones to, which right there can affect your sexual responses. Again, women are all different and I am just speaking from personal experiences with meds.

Interesting creatures

Women

Unpredictable

~Ann Gillie

CHAPTER 7

My Public Speaking

My Mission - My Goal

To be able to attend and speak at local, national and international Epilepsy events, seminars, conferences and forums on the topic of Epilepsy; but as a survivor not as a medical professional.

Forums and Media Speaking Experience

These are a few of the speaking engagements I have participated in and loved every second of every one of them!

October 2011: Calgary Epilepsy Association

I spoke in Calgary, Alberta about my experience with seizures, medications and my 1ˢᵗ book *If Walls Could Talk: Don't let epilepsy control you!*

December 2010: Interview with **Shaw TV** Edmonton on location at the U of A Hospital in Edmonton where I had my surgery, interview was also with my neurologist.

June 2010: Breakfast Television Edmonton

I was speaking about my recently published book If Walls Could Talk, as well promoting the Edmonton Epilepsy Associations 50 year anniversary.

April 2010: Arizona Epilepsy Association Walk - I was a guest speaker for the 2010 walk in Phoenix, Arizona. I spoke to over 1100 people on my Experience with seizures, my surgery and my recently published book, If Walls Could Talk: Don't let epilepsy control you!

March 2010: Glenrose Hospital Auditorium - Partnership with the University of Alberta Hospital and the Edmonton Epilepsy Association - Speaker for **Seizures and Surgery** (along side my neurosurgeon)

March 2009: Glenrose Hospital Auditorium - Partnership with the University of Alberta Hospital and the Edmonton Epilepsy Association - Speaker for "**Sex and Seizures**"

March 2007: Breakfast Television Edmonton and Global News Edmonton

I was a guest on both t.v. news stations in Mar 07 to speak about my experience with Epilepsy, provide educational information to the public andpromote Epilepsy Awareness month.

March/April 2007: Your Health Magazine (Capital Health – Edmonton and area) My story "**Seizing Life**" was published.

March 2005: Glenrose Hospital Auditorium - Partnership with the University of Alberta Hospital and the Edmonton Epilepsy Association

Speaker for "**Living with Epilepsy**"

SHAW TV Edmonton
Interview at the U of A Hospital
Dec 2009

MY WEBSITE

www.anngillieepilepsyspeaker.com

Includes:

About me

Photo Gallery

My Book

Public Speaking

Epilepsy information

Book Reviews

Edmonton Breakfast Television interview 2010

And

Contact info

Topics of Discussion for my Public Speaking

- Life with Epilepsy - child hood, teenager, adult
- The testing process I went through to see if I qualified for surgery
- The Surgery
- Recovery from surgery - memory, depression, family/friends
- Being a mother that has epilepsy
- Sex and Seizures
- Motivate others to stay positive

I want to stay positive in all my speaking engagements!

A couple of my interviews are also available on YOUTUBE

This was posted on the ***Epilepsy Canada*** website in 2011!

Spotlight on the Need for More Research

Ann Marie Gillie, a 41 year-old mother of 3 boys, is a published author and had lived with epilepsy for half of her life. A second opinion by a neurosurgeon changed her life.

In December 2002, she underwent Left Selective Amygdalohippocampectomy surgery at the University of Alberta Hospital. Ann has been 100% seizure-free since. She travels to the U.S. and across Canada to speak about her experiences and motivates others to stay positive.

If you would like to engage with Ann, you can visit her website at http://www.anngillieepilepsyspeaker.com/ Learn more about her experiences in her book called *'If Walls Could Talk – Don't Let Epilepsy Control You'.*

My book signing City Hall in Edmonton, Alberta, Canada

CHAPTER 8

Positive Reflections

I was sitting on my couch, having another French vanilla coffee, enjoying the quiet. The two oldest must have been in school and Nathan glued to a game, movie or his hot wheels cars; I was thinking back to the beginning of all of this for me. Way back to when I was little, when seizures entered my life, how I coped as a child, teen and adult with epilepsy. It was definitely a journey and a bumpy one at times for sure. In my first book I touched on some topics that made for great conversations afterwards, topics like sex and seizures, surgery and depression. Yes those can be touchy topics, but it is also good to get it out there on the table sometimes, hear it from someone else or maybe just having someone listening to you is all you need.

Well after *If Walls Could Talk* came out I loved the in-depth conversations I read or was involved with myself on my Facebook group. I am going to repeat this as many times as possible if that is what it takes for people to get the picture. YOU NEED TO TALK…. People are sometimes afraid that what they are going through or have to say is not what others want to hear, but you would be amazed; when I had an email on Facebook say to me *"wow, thanks for sharing your story with us, I really thought I was alone. I had never talked with others that know what I am going through, this is an amazing feeling and I don't feel bottled up anymore"*.

That right there made me realize that sometimes it only takes one person.

To just touch a bit on my first book, I have to say that the writing of it and having the response I did from others was probably the best therapy I could have asked for. I don't dwell on the depression I went through after my surgery anymore; I look at it now as a life altering experience. It was something that I had no control over.

My last seizures were a few days before my surgery and to this day I have not even had one! That is an accomplishment if you ask me. As far as what I am doing now and where I am, I mentioned in the beginning of the book about how positive things are for me now, work, family and speaking. I did end *If Walls Could Talk* by saying that maybe politics was in my near future. Well I have to tell you, I sure tried my hardest. I put my name in on the nomination list for City Council in Spruce Grove Alberta where I live, never running for anything like this ever before. I wasn't even nervous, which some found strange; but we are talking me here, I was excited before being put under for brain surgery.

Well I did all my own campaigning, signs, brochures and spoke at several forums, the experience was just what I hoped it would be, positive! I did not get voted in on council but it was something that I will never regret trying and who knows I have ALL my election signs VOTE ANN GILLIE FOR ALDERMAN neatly put away in my garage, it is only a year and a half away from elections again. My point is, if you want it you have to go for it, you may not win or get exactly what you want, but if you never try than you will never know. I am proud of what I did, the campaigning door to door, speaking like me not like someone I wasn't. I even had a gentleman come up to me after one of the forums and say " *You were very refreshing to listen to*", I have to tell you I think I smiled for weeks after being told that.

Life can be full of obstacles, curves and even brick walls sometimes, but if you don't make the effort to jump over those obstacles and move with those curves, even take a hammer to those walls you can't say you tried. I know that I have a lot to look forward to in my future and I plan on doing my best to accomplish even great hurdles in my life.

Epilepsy Crossword Puzzle

ANN'S WORD SEARCH

```
R  C  I  N  O  R  H  C  Y  T  E  I  X  N  A
O  S  P  A  L  O  T  E  R  G  E  T  I  R  M
I  T  E  N  O  I  S  S  E  R  P  E  D  B  Y
V  R  T  H  N  D  I  S  O  R  D  E  R  I  S
A  E  I  X  M  T  N  E  M  T  A  E  R  T  P
H  S  T  A  T  U  S  E  R  U  Z  I  E  S  E
E  S  L  N  E  U  R  O  L  O  G  Y  B  I  L
B  H  I  P  P  O  C  A  M  P  U  S  O  L  I
S  U  R  V  I  V  O  R  S  I  M  P  L  E  P
K  Z  M  C  S  I  S  O  N  G  A  I  D  J  E
O  N  O  I  T  A  C  I  N  U  M  M  O  C  C
L  O  O  S  N  O  I  T  A  C  I  D  E  M  Z
```

anxiety	epilepsy	petit
behavior	hippocampus	seizures
chronic	lobe	simple
communication	mal	stress
depression	medications	survivor
diagnosis	mri	tegretol
disorder	neurology	treatment

About the Author

I have come a long way in my life in the past nine years. I went through neuro surgery, went back to school, changed careers and became inspired to public speak about my experiences with epilepsy. I also published not one but now two books and I feel like I was supposed to take on this role of helper, healer, motivator; however one wants to view it for themselves.

Of course I have had struggles, as most do within their journey in life, but sometimes these struggles and obstacles are what inspire us to take on new directions. I am going to continue to be a positive role model when it comes to epilepsy, just hearing one person say, "thank you" will make it all worthwhile for me! On that note I would like to thank everyone who shared their stories, answers and comments with me; I think you are all an inspiration to the world.

Ann Marie Gillie

This is the poem that I wrote a few years back that inspired me to write my first book *If Walls Could Talk!*

IF WALLS COULD TALK
By: Ann Marie Gillie

They see us from all angles
Every step we take
Sleeping, talking, cleaning house
Even times we ache
They catch us sneaking cookies
Or kissing in the dark
They help us hang our pictures
And let us decorate them with art
We sometimes rough them up a bit
Even color them real bright
Punch holes and add new windows
To make an old room a new sight
If only they could tell us
The things that they have seen
A wall could write a million books
I wonder if they dream
So as you walk around your home
And gaze at your walls
Remember if a wall could talk
The fun could end for all

Acknowledgements

I obtained information for this book from

Epilepsy Canada, my Facebook Epilepsy Support Group and my own personal experiences.

Thank you to Monique, Stacey, Karl, Sarah, Narelle, Dana, Helen and Paul that took the time to sit down and put their thoughts, comments and ideas on paper for me, you are truly amazing individuals!!

We all made a great team putting this book together.
Ann Gillie

Please see my Facebook Epilepsy Support Group…
Life after brain surgery

CPSIA information can be obtained at www.ICGtesting.com
Printed in the USA
LVOW07s1451300615

443982LV00001BA/12/P